Do Plastic Surgeons Take VISA?

AND OTHER CONFESSIONS *of a* DESPERATE WOMAN

Do Plastic Surgeons Take VISA?

And Other Confessions of a Desperate Woman

Kathy Peel

WORD PUBLISHING

Dallas · London · Vancouver · Melbourne

Library of Congress Cataloging-in-Publication Data:

Peel, Kathy, 1951-
    Do plastic surgeons take Visa? and other confessions of a desperate woman / Kathy Peel.
        p.   cm.
    ISBN 0–8499–3348–X
        1. Women—Psychology.   2. Women—Religious life.   3. Marriage—Psychological aspects. 4. Mothers—Psychology.   I. Title
    HQ1206.P423   1992
    248.8'43—dc20   92—11710
                                                                                          CIP

2 3 4 9 LB 9 8 7 6 5 4 3 2 1
Printed in the United States of America

For Bill
who champions my cause

Contents

Part 4
Confessions of a Desperate Disciple

Accounts Outstanding

I'm deeply indebted to many friends and family members whose contributions I acknowledge with great joy:

John, Joel, and James Peel, my three sons, who taught me to laugh at myself;

Morris and Kathryn Weeks, my parents, and Marsha Chay, my sister, who are not surprised I wrote this book;

Peggy Zadina and Judie Byrd, loyal, long-time friends;

Dan Johnson and The Idea Agency, partners in creativity;

Steve and Debbie Keuer, loving, stand-by-me friends;

Lee and Alan Clay, Michael and Ceil Edwards, Frank and Sue Pillsbury, David and Kathryn Waldrep, and the staff at Focus on the Family, all generous and supportive friends;

Kip Jordon and the team at Word Publishing, who believe in me;

Jan Johnson, my editor, whose expertise and personal involvement added immeasurably to this book.

Introduction

There's nothing quite as embarrassing as a visit to the hospital. During this particular stint, I finished the preliminary temperature and blood pressure checks and carried out the obligatory "filling of the little cup." I stripped down to my hospital bracelet, and donned the one-size-fits-nobody hospital gown. As I walked down the radiology corridor, I nonchalantly positioned my left arm across my jiggling chest. I used my right hand to hold the back opening together—hoping my south end was not on display to the world. As I approached the examination room, I passed a proctologist and froze—fanny against the wall. I didn't want him to get any ideas.

I sprawled on a cold examination table, and five doctors took turns working over my body. As they each poked on their particular area of expertise, they threw around letters in important sounding ways. "Schedule a CAT, an IVP, a BAER, and a UGI, and give us the results of her EEG, EKG, EMG, and LP, ASAP." I wondered if they learned any real words in medical school.

The memory of these men of science twisting and turning my body into unfeminine contortions far surpasses any other recollections I have of being totally humiliated. But I felt so lousy that day that modesty was the last thing on my mind. As the bewildered physicians scratched their heads, I was afraid they had come to the conclusion that my body needed to be donated to the nearest medical school. I was sick, and I was scared. You might say that I was a desperate woman.

When the test results were in, I was diagnosed with chronic mononucleosis syndrome. (Today this is called chronic fatigue syndrome.) There was nothing much they could do for me. I returned home still completely drained of energy and unable to think clearly or function without pain. During the six hours a day I managed to hold my eyes open, I did a lot of thinking and praying.

God has used some interesting methods over the years to get my attention. When he ordains a "pause" in my life—a quiet time for reflecting on my direction, revising my priorities and revamping my schedule—I go kicking and screaming all the way, like a child going to the doctor for a shot. "I don't have time to be sick," I grumble. "I've got too much to do!" It seems he always has to go to great extremes to get me to settle down and listen. During this particular thirty-something pause, he got my undivided attention. I *was* a desperate woman.

Through that experience I became a die-hard believer in the old adage that one never appreciates something until it is taken away. Ordinary living took on new meaning for me. I thought: "If only I felt like changing my baby's diaper. If only I could cook dinner. If only I had the energy to exercise. If only I felt like planning a late-night rendezvous with my husband." I was overwhelmed by my inability to carry on with my life. Things that once fell into the category of duties became privileges I dearly missed. Even the pleasures of life required what seemed to be a superhuman effort.

Now I hate to confess to being the sort of person who tries to wager with God, but I admit I wanted to take him to the bargaining table and strike a deal. I thought seriously about praying: "Lord, if you'll just let me feel good again, I promise to appreciate every single day and not gripe about anything, ever again." How God must tenderly chuckle at the schemes of his children when we think we can dicker with our Creator. When I saw the stupidity of my scheme, I took comfort in realizing that

God knows me better than I know myself. He loves me, forgives me, and continues to lead me even when I want to make promises I can't fulfill.

Despite my self-centeredness and crude understanding of theology, God graciously restored my health and energy. I came out on the other side of a long, dark tunnel of illness with a renewed passion to live each day to the fullest; to strive to become all that God created me to be in every area of my life; and to live in a manner worthy of the position I've been given in God's family. I also came away with the realization that I am an immensely selfish person who has a huge capacity for sin—totally inadequate in and of myself to pull off any lasting change of character. I was keenly aware of my desperate need for help.

This book contains the confessions of a desperate woman. Actually I don't believe I'm unique. I think we're all desperately needy people, whether we know it or not. And when we acknowledge our helplessness, God meets us at our points of desperation in unique and individual ways.

I'm not offering any magic tricks in this book that will transform you overnight, nor do I recommend a "Sure-fire, Follow-These-Steps-to-Glory" formula. I don't have an 800 number you can call to send in your $19.95 for a kit that will solve all your problems. What I do have—and it's something that every Christian woman has—is this:

1. a heavenly Father who has begun a good work in me and, despite my sinfulness, is absolutely committed to transforming my character into the likeness of Jesus Christ,

2. a living Savior who has promised to be my daily deliverer from sin's dominion,

3. an indwelling Holy Spirit who empowers me to do God's will,

4. the promises in God's Word that guide me to know what is excellent,

5. fourteen hundred and forty minutes each day in which I choose how I'm going to live, and

6. enough problems to keep me challenged on a daily basis.

Although God has helped me incorporate many disciplines into my days that have brought my life into clearer focus and given me a much richer and more abundant life than I ever imagined, please don't get the idea that I have "arrived." As a matter of fact, it's only a matter of time before my family writes the book *Coping with a Desperate Woman*. They certainly won't be short on real-life stories. Just my behavior today could fill a whole chapter.

"Boys, Mom had a hard day," Bill covered for me graciously. "Let's all be extra nice to her tonight. She just needs to rest." (Which translated means: "Hey guys, red alert on Mom tonight. You'd best steer clear or she might bite your head off. I'll see if I can get her to go to bed early.")

I knew it was true. Today my personality left a lot to be desired—like distance. As I stared at the deep frown lines in my face, I looked like a constipation commercial. I tried to rationalize that it was the twenty-first day of my monthly cycle (or did I use that excuse on the seventh day and the fourteenth day?). "How in the fat," I scoffed silently at myself, "could you—the Desperado Queen— even entertain the thought of writing a book to help other women who feel desperate? What a joke!" At that point my cynicism turned to tears.

By nature, I am a fighter who hates for anything to get the best of me—especially a horrible mood. I knew I needed to change my perspective and rise above my ugly disposition. "Lord," I knelt and prayed silently, "I'm miserable and I'm making everyone else miserable. I don't even know what to pray. Please help me. I'm a desperate woman."

"Okay," I got up and stated aloud with resolve, "I need to be proactive about this. Just sitting around moping never helps." I thoughtfully paced back and forth across the bedroom. "I've got it . . . I need to *read* something to get my thoughts moving in a positive direction." I glanced over a shelf full of books. "Maybe a humorous book," I decided. "I need a good laugh." I opened a book and began thumbing through it. "No, this is a serious problem. What I really need is spiritual help . . . perhaps a devotional book." I found one, then sat down and started to read. "But, I'm tired and out of ideas. I want to read a practical book that can give me some specific actions to take. I wish there were a humorous, but helpful book by a woman I can relate to who has real problems."

Well, even though, as the kids say, "the lights were on and the dogs were barking," the truth of what was happening at that moment finally hit me. Crying and laughing at the same time, I cried out, "I'm writing the book I want to read!"

I hope as you read my book you will laugh with me and at me—and perhaps learn to laugh at yourself. I also hope you will entertain the possibility of a loving and caring God who is daily meeting your needs at your own unique points of desperation. At the end of each chapter I have listed various daily disciplines—expressions of who I am, what I think, how I look, what I do, what I eat, and how I feel. Use these ideas as springboards as you think about your life and circumstances—to write your own self-disciplines. Depending on where you are in your personal pilgrimage, you may want to choose one or more to think about or incorporate into your life. They're only suggestions to get you going.

Please don't think you must do them all! If this book puts you on a guilt trip, I have failed. If you come away saying, "I give up; I could never do that," then we've both wasted our time. But if you are somehow motivated to allow God to do big things in your life, to pull you out of the mire of mediocrity in some area, to push you onward and upward to a new plateau, then I have fulfilled my purpose.

Part 1

Confessions of a Desperate Woman

1

Do Plastic Surgeons Take Visa?

"Mommy, did you know your legs are lumpy like cottage cheese?"

Six-year-old James broadcast his observation to the entire shallow end of the swimming pool. Even the lifeguard glanced down our way to see if he could spot this strange phenomenon. I just smiled at him and the twenty-something mothers whose toned and tanned bodies were posed poolside. I'd like to see what they look like at forty, I thought snidely as I slipped into the pool hoping to hide my prominent thighs. Nevertheless, I had a feeling it was going to be a long summer.

James's comment spurred me on. Weight control is a constant battle for me, but I'm committed to keep fighting. I sincerely believe God wants us to take care of ourselves—to look and feel our best. And I feel better about myself when I take care of my body. So that afternoon I decided it was time to take inventory—from the top down. I wanted to know just what I had to work with. I locked the bedroom door and started my evaluation at my dressing table. As I traced the lines and crevices across my face, my hopes that the kids had overlaid a map of the Mississippi and its tributaries on the makeup mirror vanished. My twice-a-day Queen Esther routine was obviously not working. The cabinet full of anti-age, nonwrinkle, rejuvenating creams had delivered minimal results, and I was now codependent on Oil of Olay.

I then mustered up every ounce of courage within me and stood stark naked in front of a full-length mirror. It was a scary sight. Twenty years and three children since my wedding day, and my chest gave new meaning to the word "swags." Not only that, they were swags for a very small drape. Suddenly the term "breast augmentation" took on new significance. I calculated that if I clipped coupons for the next nine years and pocketed the money, I could save enough to have one breast enlarged. I decided that an uplifting padded bra would be a much more *balanced* approach and less risky.

Glancing down at my tummy and thighs was quite a shock to my system as well. Why, pray tell, was I not born during the Renaissance when plump, pear-shaped bodies were in vogue? I could have easily been the centerfold for *Seventeenth Century Woman* magazine. But no . . . I have to live at the end of the twentieth century when anyone wider than a popsicle stick qualifies for a liquid diet commercial.

As I continued my evaluation, I confessed my whining and decided to take a spiritual approach to the problem of getting back into shape. I wondered what God would think of liposuction. I searched my Bible and found the verse "woe . . . to them that give suck. . . ." Now I know that verse from Matthew 24 wasn't written about liposuction. But it made sense in a quirky sort of way. So I decided I'd best try a different angle. Maybe a girdle would work—a silent one that wouldn't screech when my thighs rub together.

I finished the assessment with a panoramic view of my hair style—which had the appearance of a heavy traffic path in shag carpet. My kids called it my "matted poodle" look. When I asked my hair stylist to give me a new young look, I didn't know that to create this "care-free" style I'd have to spend forty-five minutes using a diffuser, three types of hair picks, two sizes of round brushes, hot rollers, duckbill clips, mousse, and spritzer, only to look as if I'd just survived a tornado.

As much as I hated to admit it, when I scanned the perimeter of my middle-aged body, I knew I was dealing with a long-range project. With determination not to let this get me down, I got dressed. I heard a knock on my door. "Mom, are you okay in there?" I opened the door and tried to bolster my self-image by fishing for a compliment. "Guys, did I ever tell you I was once in a beauty contest with Cybill Shepherd?" They rolled their eyes and responded, "You've told us that story at least twenty times, and we still want to send it to *Ripley's Believe It or Not.*"

After threatening to discontinue their allowance, I indignantly reminded them that I take care of my body. I sucked in my stomach and continued, "I'm looking pretty sharp for a forty-one-year-old woman. I can still get into most of my size-eight skirts and, lucky for you, I haven't dipped into your college fund to get my eyelids done."

I thought for sure they would fall prostrate at my feet and call me blessed. Instead they dug into their repertoire of family barbs and started in with flabby-arm-waving jokes and "Did the Flood occur before or after you were born?" comments. John philosophically added, "Gosh, I bet I'm the only kid on earth with a mom whose hair color and skin color both come out of a bottle. Mom, give it up. It's a little late for the California-girl look."

I was thankful I'd passed the stage of allowing my children's jokes to determine my self-esteem. I played along with them and we had a good laugh. But inwardly I knew it wasn't getting any easier to keep the makeup from caking in the creases and the pounds from creeping up on the scales.

I find nothing wrong with wanting to look nice and maximize the "equipment" God gave me. I am the King of kings' royal representative on earth, and I want to represent him in the loveliest way I can. I also want my family to be proud of me. And I want to be my best for myself too. When I feel good about how I look and feel, I'm free to love and give myself to others. I accomplish a lot more too.

But early in my pilgrimage toward adulthood, I followed the path of modern American culture and took this mind-set to an unhealthy extreme. An unbalanced view of the importance of my appearance led to incorrect perceptions and to a very dark period in my life. I had to learn the hard way the importance of seeking God's perspective on this issue. It is not without embarrassment that I tell this story.

I really was in a beauty contest with Cybill Shepherd. She was a shoo-in for the Miss Junior Memphis contest. High cheekbones, long slender legs, flashy smile. None of the other contestants, including me, even came close to her natural beauty. So it was no surprise when she walked away with the trophy. But something happened inside me when I lost that pageant. I began to concentrate on the fact that I would never be a beauty queen. I carried this to the extreme of doubting my self-worth. Why was I built so low to the ground? Would my body ever stretch out so I'd have legs like Ginger Rogers's? And my hair . . . why was it so curly? I wanted the straight stringy look of the Yardley models then in vogue. In short, I wanted to be somebody other than the Kathy whom God made. And I wanted to be her so badly that I had real trouble living with the Kathy whom God did make.

Since my mom owned two of the most popular dress shops in Memphis, it was easy for me to coordinate perfectly put-together outfits—hoping to cover up the fact that I didn't really like what the clothes were hiding underneath. When I moved into the dorm at Southern Methodist University in Dallas, my roommate couldn't believe the extent of my wardrobe. Not only would my clothes and accessories not fit in the closet and drawers, it was no small chore trying to cram forty pairs of shoes on a rack intended for five pairs.

Although I became a Christian through the ministry of Young Life in high school, I did what many freshmen college students do. I lived with one foot in the spiritual world and the other foot in the party world. I majored in social science (heavy on the social) and early on declared a minor in beer and bridge. I also ate my fair share of pretzels, potato chips, and pizza—almost every night at the bridge table. On the eat-as-you-play plan, it only took me one semester to gain twenty pounds.

Talk about miserable. I decided the weight had to go—one way or another. So I pursued what I thought was a normal plan of action. I took diet pills.

For one month I functioned in hyperdrive and ate nothing but lettuce and diet pills. I ended up in the campus infirmary, but didn't care. I lost twenty pounds in thirty days and that's what mattered. My miniskirts looked great again.

One weekend after my crash diet, I invited a friend who had also been dieting to celebrate our weight loss. We went out for a night on the town and ate our way through Dallas. Pizza, pastries, pies . . . you name it, we ate it. We literally stuffed our size-six "hot pants" until we were nauseated.

When we arrived back at the dorm, I remember walking into the restroom thinking, "I feel like I need to throw up." Very innocently, I stuck my finger down my throat to start the process. Five minutes later my stomach was empty.

The next morning I got up and went through my usual ritual of shuffling to the bathroom, brushing my teeth, and checking my profile to measure the flatness of my tummy. It was flat. Flat! I couldn't believe it. After all the delicious food we had enjoyed the night before, my stomach was flat! I actually thought I had discovered a new approach to dieting—eat all you want, then throw up. Unpleasant, but very effective.

Well, that's how it started. I understand that part. But I can't explain to you in medical or psychological terms, how an innocent act led to a horrible addiction. Although I'd never even heard the word bulimia, the ritual of eating and purging became my regular method of dealing with stress.

About that time, I started attending a Bible study and a good church. My spiritual life blossomed as God drew me unto himself, and I hungered to know him more. But the more light he shed on my life, the darker this secret sin became to me. I certainly couldn't share it with anyone. That's part of the sin and the sickness of addiction. We keep secrets when we're addicted. We live in fear that someone will find out we're not perfect. The longer we keep the secret, the more fraudulent we feel. And that leads to more secret keeping, worsening the cycle.

Also about this time I met a wonderful Christian boy. Bill and I married the summer before our senior year at SMU. As we grew in our relationship with God and each other, I appeared to be the perfect Christian wife—encouraging my husband through seminary, then playing the supportive assistant pastor's wife role at a large church. But behind the scenes, all was not well.

Because I was in bondage to a life-threatening addiction, I lived under a heavy load of guilt. Every part of my being throbbed with shame. I was unable to love myself, and this made it impossible to love my family and others as I should.

Finally I came to a point of desperation. I read everything I could about bulimia and searched the scriptures diligently for answers. I personalized every verse I could find on God's deliverance, his power, his love, and the Holy Spirit's sanctifying work in my life. I knew that if indeed I did believe in a God who is powerful enough to save me from my sins and give me eternal life, he'd better be able to save me from this sin that could very well send me to an early death.

Six months and eight spiral notebooks later, three specific verses stood out in my mind. I wrote down the verses and the action I felt I should take in response.

> Therefore confess your sins to each other and pray for each other so that you may be healed. The prayer of a righteous man is powerful and effective.
>
> James 5:16

I knew I needed to confess my addiction and become accountable to someone committed to helping me and praying for me. In my case, my husband became this person.

> Then they cried to the Lord in their trouble,
>   and he saved them from their distress.
> He sent forth his word and healed them;
>   he rescued them from the grave.
>   Psalm 107:19–20

I believed that somehow God would use his word to save me from this heinous sin. I did not know how he would do this, but I made a commitment to continue to drench myself daily in scripture.

For though we live in the world, we do not wage war as the world does. The weapons we fight with are not the weapons of the world. On the contrary, they have divine power to demolish strongholds. We demolish arguments and every pretension that sets itself up against the knowledge of God, and we take captive every thought to make it obedient to Christ.

2 Corinthians 10:3–5

This verse made me really mad. I realized I'd been snookered! I had fought a battle for over ten years. I was losing—and I don't like to lose anything! On the battlefield of my mind, Satan, the father of lies, had set up arguments and pretensions—that I was hopelessly bulimic and thus worthless to God or anyone else; that I could never get better and was thus even more worthless; and that God would help only a better person—not me. These thoughts were totally against my knowledge of God—that Christ is my daily deliverer from sin's dominion and I am no longer a slave to sin.

Although I carried out my daily duties as usual, I thought frequently about these verses and how I could specifically apply their principles to my problem. Then at three o'clock in the morning I awoke—keenly aware that the battle going on in my mind was for my life. I tiptoed into our family room, sat down on the sofa, and opened my Bible to 2 Corinthians 10:3–5. I prayed that God would fight this battle for me, that he would be my strength and my deliverer.

I cannot explain what exactly happened, but at some point during the next few minutes I knew that God used my belief in the truth of these verses from 2 Corinthians to end my battle against bulimia. My entire way of seeing the problem took a 180-degree turn. I realized I was not hopelessly bulimic or unworthy of God's help. I experienced his love and power in a way I never knew before. Not knowing quite how to respond, I expressed my feelings by writing this prayer in my journal:

> The battle is won
>> Your grace has overcome
> Satan has fled
>> You fill me instead
> With power, peace, and love.

For the first time I understood what Jesus meant when he said: "Then you will know the truth, and the truth will set you free" (John 8:32). I softly cried tears of joy, knowing I would never suffer from bulimia again. I fell asleep holding my Bible and prayer journal.

The next day was Saturday. We did our usual Saturday chores as a family, but I knew things weren't *usual*. I felt a freedom I had never before experienced. A freedom to eat wisely, to like myself, and to love my husband and children in deeper ways.

That night, as is our custom, I went into three-year-old Joel's bedroom to sing hymns and pray before bed. The words of Charles Wesley's hymn "And Can It Be" came to mind, and I began singing quietly. When I came to the third verse, tears of joy rolled down my cheeks. I now intimately understood the meaning of the words.

> Long my imprisoned spirit lay
>> Fast bound in sin and nature's night
> Thine eye diffused a quick'ning ray,
>> I woke, the dungeon flamed with light;
> My chains fell off, My heart was free;
>> I rose, went forth, and followed Thee.

Joel touched my damp cheek and asked me why I was so sad. I smiled and answered, "I'm not sad, Darling. I'm crying because I'm happy—so happy to be free."

Knowing he didn't understand, I kissed him gently and tucked him in.

Weight control will always be a struggle for me, as it is for so many women. A dear friend and former college roommate, Kathryn Waldrep, practices obstetrics and gynecology in Dallas. She says that almost every one of her patients over the age of forty automatically gains five pounds each year because of metabolism slowdown. If this distressing trend is inevitable, it seems that we have three possible responses: We can buy clothing with elastic waistbands—then sit back and let it happen. We can try extreme, expensive, unhealthy weight-loss plans—which, by the way, almost guarantee that you will gain back the weight you lose within a year. Or we can commit to fighting the battle wisely with God's help through discipline, regular exercise, and sensible eating habits.

We also need to make sure our definition of "good figure" is accurate. So many women—young or older—are dissatisfied with their bodies because they want to look like a media image. Let's face it—very few of us have perfect "10" bodies. We take a giant step toward a healthy self-image when we give up this delusion and begin to love ourselves as daughters of God—as he intended.

I still believe that it is important to look my best externally and make the most of the raw materials God gave me to work with. I do this for my Lord, for my husband, and for myself. When I feel good about myself I can be a better disciple . . . more others-centered instead of me-centered. When I take care of my body I feel more lovely, and I'm able to love my husband more freely. And when I walk past a mirror and enjoy who's looking back at me, I am invigorated and more productive. It's a satisfying feeling to know that even though I'm nowhere near perfect and never will be, I'm trying to maximize the potential of how God made me.

I try to look my best also for my kids. I learned this last one from my mother when I was young. Sloppy has never been a word in her vocabulary. I'll never forget the day she and three other mothers helped with my third-grade party. Mom took the time to fix herself up, while the other moms came to school looking unkempt and frumpy. The cutest boy in the class leaned across the aisle to my desk and said, "Gosh, your mom sure is neat." I felt so proud!

But there's something much more important than taking time and effort to make our outer being as lovely as possible. We can tighten our stomach muscles and suck it up, pay a plastic surgeon to tuck it up, or spend a lot of money trying to dress it up, but unless we are growing beautiful on the inside, our efforts to be glamorous on the outside are useless. Proverbs 11:22 says: "Like a gold ring in a pig's snout is a beautiful woman who shows no discretion." And Proverbs 31:30 states: "Charm is deceptive, and beauty is fleeting; but a woman who fears the Lord is to be praised."

There's a balance between external and internal beauty that we must search for *individually* as we seek to reach the full potential of what God created us to be. What's right for some will be wrong for others. What works for one will backfire on the next. We're each unique. I learned this through a humbling experience.

I was asked to be involved in a project with a woman from California. When I was introduced to her, I thought to myself, This dear lady needs my help! Hmmm . . . a little makeup, a change of hair style—maybe even a little color, and definitely a more flattering wardrobe. I'll bet God has allowed our paths to cross so he can use me in her life to help her become more attractive.

After spending a week with her, I felt totally humiliated. I decided that, without a doubt, she was the most beautiful woman I had ever met. Although she wore no makeup and her clothes were dated, she radiated a beauty from within I had never before experienced.

As we each strive in our own way to make the most of our personal appearance, let us never forget what's most important—that it is God's will for each of us to become like Jesus Christ, the loveliest creature of all.

Daily Disciplines

"Every little bit helps." My children hate it when I say that—especially when we're playing Monopoly. While they're holding out for the big properties—waiting to be able to put hotels on Boardwalk and Park Place, I'm stockpiling the cheaper ones. I save the small bits of rent money they owe when they land on my houses in the "low-rent district," as they put it. But guess who usually wins? I do, because all the little deals add up to a big win at the end.

I think the same principle holds true for dieting and taking care of our bodies—every little bit helps. Wise behavior daily adds to overall better physical condition. Sure we can go on starvation diets and lose a lot of weight quickly. Or we can be gung-ho about a do-or-die exercise program that means a major lifestyle change. But, more often than not, drastic measures such as these don't work.

So schedule some time when you can be alone. Honestly evaluate the condition of your body and your personal habits. Write down what would have to change for you to operate at peak performance and look your best. Then look through this list of daily disciplines. They're not in any particular order. Just try a few that fit comfortably into your lifestyle. Please don't try to do them all, or you might kill yourself! Make it your overall goal to implement healthy, wise decisions every day about what you eat and drink, and how you take care of your body. At the end of the chapter there's space for you to add your disciplines and ideas.

❦ Seek out a good Christian counselor immediately if you are fighting an eating disorder.

❦ Commit yourself to a regular exercise program. Try to exercise aerobically at least three hours each week. Join an aerobic dance class, swim laps, ride a bicycle, jog, jump rope, or walk briskly on your lunch break. If you can't join a class try jumping on a mini-trampoline every morning while watching the news. Record your time and activity in an exercise diary or journal. Then reward yourself after completing a month of regular exercise.

❦ Squeeze your fanny muscles when you're riding an elevator, waiting in a long line, or caught in a traffic jam.

❦ Do deep knee bends while drying your hair.

❦ Keep three-pound weights in an easily accessible location. Use them to firm up your arm muscles two to three minutes each day.

❦ Enroll in a nutrition course or physical education class at a local college.

❦ Ask your physician to recommend a good diet and exercise program and to help you discern the weight that is healthiest for you.

❦ Float lemons in a pretty pitcher full of water. Drink six to eight glasses every day. If you work, take a favorite glass to keep on your desk. Refill it with fresh water regularly.

❦ Try to let your digestive tract rest for twelve hours each day. If you eat breakfast at 7:00 A.M., don't eat after 7:00 P.M. the night before.

❦ Purchase a small inexpensive cotton rug or exercise mat. Start slowly and work up to fifty sit-ups each day.

❦ Buy a small stepstool with rubber-tipped legs so it won't slip. Step up and down 100 times. This is great for your gluteus muscles.

❦ Take vitamins daily.

❦ Limit your sugar intake. (I allow myself six sugary desserts each year. I save these for special occasions or dinner parties.)

❦ Meditate on this verse: "Don't you know that you yourselves are God's temple and that God's Spirit lives in you?" (1 Cor. 3:16).

❦ Practice good posture. Try to walk through your house with a book balanced on top of your head.

❦ Get plenty of sleep.

❦ Eat more complex carbohydrates. They fill you up without overloading your system with calories.

❦ Do floor exercises while watching an old movie.

❦ Eat slowly. Put your fork down between each bite. Studies show that most overweight people eat very fast. Never clean your plate.

❦ Exercise with your family in fun ways. Take a bike hike, throw a Frisbee, have a sit-ups contest or a family softball game.

❦ Keep fresh vegetables cut up in your refrigerator.

❦ Don't eat standing up. Cows graze.

❦ Play calm background music while you eat. Research shows that listening to fast music causes us to eat faster.

❦ Buy a calorie counting book and use it daily. Keep a pad of paper and pencil in the kitchen handy. It's easy to take in more than you realize.

❦ Grab a piece of fruit when you're hungry.

❦ Enroll in a dance class that you've always dreamed of. One friend began ballet at the age of thirty. I started tap dancing at forty!

❦ Take a brisk (three miles per hour) fifteen-minute walk. You'll burn sixty calories and feel invigorated.

❦ Decrease your fat intake. Use just enough low-fat margarine to taste on bread or rolls. Try plain, low-fat yogurt on a baked potato instead of butter and sour cream.

❦ Take the stairs whenever possible.

❦ Don't keep your favorite junk foods around the house.

❦ Only allow yourself three small bites of a recipe you have to taste to get the seasoning right.

❦ Install a full-length mirror in your bedroom or bath.

❦ Wear tennis shoes when doing housework. Go about your work with an "attitude of exercise." Bend, stretch, and move briskly.

❦ Turn Romans 6:1–14 into a personal prayer. Write down the verses substituting your name or "I" for each personal pronoun.

❦ Don't always look for the closest parking place at the mall. The walk will do you good.

❦ Buy one-pound weights and just wear them on your wrists or ankles when you're puttering around the house.

❦ "We make a ladder of our vices if we trample those same vices underfoot"—Saint Augustine. What does this quote mean to you?

❦ Find some good music on the radio and do isometric arm exercises in the car when on a long trip.

❦ Don't have unrealistic expectations. Diet wisely.

❦ Take long strides and tighten your thigh and hip muscles when walking through an airport.

❦ Drink skim milk instead of whole or 2 percent.

❦ Find a friend and be mutually accountable to each other about what you eat and how much you exercise.

❦ Enjoy a fruit juice spritzer. Mix one-third of a cup of fruit juice with Diet Sprite.

❦ Keep lotion in various locations so you can moisturize your skin when you have a couple of extra minutes. I keep lotion in my car, purse, kitchen drawer, bedside table, and bathrooms.

❦ Have your makeup done once by a professional cosmetologist. Let her show you how to bring out your best features.

❦ Give yourself a facial once a week. Clean skin is healthier skin.

❦ Invest in a well-lit magnifying makeup mirror and a good pair of tweezers. (These two items are a premenopausal woman's best friends!) Keep unwanted hairs plucked regularly. Have heavy or dark facial hair professionally waxed.

❦ Brush your teeth once a week with baking soda. This helps clean away coffee and tea stains.

❦ Keep an emergency makeup kit in your car or briefcase to quickly freshen up.

❦ Have a hair stylist study the shape of your face and help you decide what length and shape is best for you.

❦ Ask a good friend to be really honest with you about what styles and shapes look best on your body. You can appear to gain or lose ten pounds by the clothes you wear.

❦ Learn which colors look best on you. Some gals look radiant in warm, earthy colors. They coordinate their wardrobe around brown accessories. Others look sophisticated as they revolve outfits around black. Most of my wardrobe goes with navy accessories. I like to wear bright colors—they tend to energize me. I've found that on days when I'm feeling sluggish, I feel better if I put on brightly colored clothes.

❦ Shop wisely for clothes. Stay away from fads. I'm a big believer in the old adage "you get what you pay for." I'd rather buy one really nice outfit rather than three cheap outfits that fall apart after six months. Good clothes with classic lines last a long time. The same holds true for purses and shoes. I just threw away a pair of good leather shoes I'd worn for eleven years.

❦ Read 1 Peter 3:3–5. Jot down thoughts about what these verses mean to you.

Self-Disciplines

❦ To get you started, think about this: First you make your decisions, then your decisions make you. Does it tell you anything about yourself? Does it bring to mind a decision you've made that rules your life? Perhaps you want to make a decision to change some aspect of your life.

2

PMS: Psychotic Mood Swings

*I*t had been a stressful day—or so I rationalized. On the way to the veterinarian, our Labrador retriever decided to make a large deposit on the back seat . . . the aroma of which caused James to throw up in the front seat. After the vet turned down my request to board them both, I went straight to a full-service carwash and hid in the restroom. (I was afraid the attendants would ask for hazardous-duty pay before touching my car.)

Then my banker called to say, "Let's do lunch!" How special, I thought. I just love personal attention. But this guy turned out to be no fun *at all*. He didn't find it one bit amusing that I tried to pay our mortgage with my credit card to earn a free trip to Florida. "Just think of it as creative accounting," I explained. He didn't smile. And I was insulted when he asked if I was on a budget. "Of course I'm on a budget," I snapped. "I never spend more than I can borrow against our life insurance."

And I paid a visit to the gynecologist for my annual checkup. You know the scene by memory. Medical schools train every gynecologist in America to walk into the examination room and immediately begin talking about the weather. Then, as they pull down the sheet to reveal your chest, they always say, "Now just relax." Right. You show me a woman who can relax while a doctor is using his fingers like a squeegee to search her breasts for rocks, and I'll show you a woman with an empty bottle of white zinfandel in her car. Then, when they put on the rubber glove, you know it's time to slip your feet into the stirrups. But because of nervous perspiration, your back is now glued to the vinyl pad. And as you shimmy your fanny down to the edge of the table it makes an embarrassing noise.

Wednesday went from bad to worse, and so did my personality. The problem was—Wednesday lasted all week. Harrison Ford could have walked through the door and I would have found something negative to say. By Friday my family was ready to lock me in the closet and slip my meals under the door. Bill, fearing for his life, gently asked me, "Honey, do you think you could be experiencing a touch of PMS?" I burst into tears. "How dare you accuse me of something so . . . so *average*. Every other woman in America has PMS. You know how I hate to be like everybody else. What a cruel thing to say!" At this point he knew he couldn't win.

The next week I was totally embarrassed by my behavior. Thankfully, Bill is a gracious guy. Trying to find humor in the situation, he wrote The PMS Rules and taped a copy to our bedroom door. The rules are more accurate than I care to confess.

The PMS Rules

1. The female always makes the rules.
2. The female has the right to change the rules at any time without prior notification.
3. The female is never wrong.
4. If the female is wrong, it is not her fault and the male must apologize to the female immediately for any complicity on his part, actual or imaginary.

5. The female has the right to plead not guilty for an action by reason of temporary insanity from PMS, and claim immunity from any consequences.

6. The male, on the other hand, must never suggest that PMS has in any way influenced the behavior of the female.

7. The male must avoid bringing up anything controversial that needs rational discussion during an "attack."

8. The male must memorize the verse "This too shall pass," but never repeat it aloud in the presence of the female.

9. Should by some cruel twist of fate the male have a bad day, he must at all costs suppress his emotions. (Ulcers are better than fingernail lacerations.)

10. If there is any disagreement about the interpretation of these rules, see rule one.

PMS or not, if I called your family right now, what would they tell me about you? Would they say you are fun to be around? Pleasant? Gracious? Patient? Or do they secretly call you the Wicked Witch of the North?

I have the privilege of meeting a wide variety of women from all over the country. We vary in education, socioeconomic level, political persuasion, and religious affiliation. But many of us have one thing in common: Although some days of the month are worse than others, we regularly struggle with keeping our personalities on an even keel. It's almost as though we have an enlarging machine in our minds that blows up the negative or difficult parts of life. This magic machine also makes things smaller—the positive parts of our life. When this happens, it is extremely difficult to maintain an attitude of contentment, which to a great extent determines our disposition. I think we inherited from Eve this tendency to let our emotions and desires dictate our behavior. We habitually choose to concentrate on what we don't have instead of consistently counting our blessings.

Can't you see her? Eve is standing at her garden kitchen window doing the dishes. (Or was she? Surely there weren't dirty dishes before the Fall!) She hums a pleasant tune as she enjoys a perfect environment, a perfect marriage, a perfect job, and a perfect walk with God. Then, suddenly, a tree in the middle of the garden captures her attention. She takes her eyes off all her blessings and focuses on the one thing she can't have.

I imagine if we stopped right now and played a few verses of "Just As I Am," there would be many of us who would need to come forward and confess, "Yes, I am just like Eve." I take my eyes off my blessings regularly and focus on the things I don't have—maybe it's something about my husband, my children, my job, my bank account, my circumstances. I forget the positives and concentrate on the negatives. And when I do, I become grumpy, critical, and discontented.

Actually, I think if we were honest we'd admit that this kind of attitude stems from a position of self-pity— you know, the old "If only . . ." disease. "If only my husband stayed home more. . . . If only my children would behave. . . . If only my nose were smaller. . . . If only we had more money. . . . If only I had a bigger house. . . ." Go ahead, try it. Make your own "If only" list.

I do it sometimes as part of a discipline. *Then* I try to finish the sentences. "If only, then what?" By the time I do two or three I usually realize how unrealistic I'm being. I'm trying to control. I'm striving for perfection from my family and myself. Most of the time I can make myself laugh. Laughter is a very good cure for self-pity.

In Matthew 16 we find the origin of self-pity. It comes straight from the pit. Remember when Jesus told his disciples he would have to suffer, die, and be raised to life again? What was Peter's response? "Never, Lord! This shall never happen to you!"

Now I don't know about you, but I think if I had been in Jesus' shoes I would have said, "You're right, Peter! Thanks for pointing that out. I *don't* deserve this. My gosh, I've lived a perfect life. *If only* I didn't have to go through with this." I think if anyone ever deserved to complain and feel sorry for himself it was Jesus. But he responded, "Get behind me, Satan!" He knew the temptation to focus on the negative and indulge in self-pity was straight from hell.

I learned a major lesson about focus from my father. On a family trip to visit my parents in Memphis, John, Joel, and I played spades with my dad at the kitchen table. Out of the blue, Joel noticed my dad's partially crippled hands. His childlike curiosity got the best of him. He asked, "Granddaddy, what's wrong with your hands?"

My dad, who never complains but has suffered with debilitating arthritis for thirty-five years, smiled and answered, "Oh, that's just my arthritis." He held out one hand and continued, "Even though these three fingers won't move, I've still got two that work fine." He wiggled the two fingers he was holding his cards between. My father has an incredible capacity to focus on the positive. He believes it is unproductive to wallow in your problems. He doesn't waste time on the dead-end belief that he deserves five good fingers. Instead he is thankful he has two and makes the most of his life.

"I want to be like that," I thought, "thankful for what's right, not bitter over what's wrong." I believe that hardships will make us either bitter or better. The determinative factor is focus. If I concentrate on what I *don't* have, I will feel empty, discontented, and resentful. But if I focus on what I do have, I will feel full, content, and grateful.

There are countless days when I forget what God has given me and find myself in a negative frame of mind because of hard circumstances. Principles from Jeremiah 29 help me turn off my problem-enlarging machine, get my thoughts on the right track, and regain a proper perspective. The prophet Jeremiah wrote a letter to the Jewish people who had been carried into exile from Jerusalem to Babylon. (Just remembering that I haven't lost my country, my home, and my freedom puts my circumstances in a little better light!) To encourage the people and give them guidance about what their response should be in the midst of an incredibly hard situation, Jeremiah wrote:

> This is what the Lord Almighty, the God of Israel, says to all those I carried into exile from Jerusalem to Babylon: "Build houses and settle down; plant gardens and eat what they produce. Marry and have sons and daughters; find wives for your sons and give your daughters in marriage, so that they too may have sons and daughters. Increase in number there; do not decrease. Also, seek the peace and prosperity of the city to which I have carried you into exile. Pray to the Lord for it, because if it prospers, you too will prosper."
>
> "For I know the plans I have for you," declares the Lord, "plans to prosper you and not to harm you, plans to give you hope and a future. Then you will call upon me and come and pray to me, and I will listen to you. You will seek me and find me when you seek me with all your heart. I will be found by you," declares the Lord.
>
> Jeremiah 29:4–7, 11–14

Let's face it, they lost a lot. But they still had God. He hadn't abandoned his people. He was there in Babylon as surely as he was in Jerusalem—and he was enough. Because of this, they could go on with life.

Hoping God won't mind my loose paraphrase, I personalized this passage and wrote it in my prayer journal like this:

> Kathy, you're in a difficult situation, hard circumstances over which you have no control. So make the best of it. Don't just sit there and complain—get on with life! Don't think like a victim, take the initiative for good. Pray about what's going on. Don't give up, and always remember God is here and has big plans for you. Use your negative circumstances to develop a closer relationship with God. He wants you to find him and know him better.

Even when my disposition seems hopelessly set in concrete, I've found one thing that begins to pry "poor me" off dead center and move me toward an attitude of contentment: remembering that this God who is with me is more powerful than anything I can imagine . . . including my moods. Just how powerful is God? Psalm 8:3–4 says "When I consider your heavens, the work of your fingers, the moon and the stars, which you have set in place, what is man that you are mindful of him, the son of man that you care for him?" I remind myself of the grandeur of the heavens God set in place—that our galaxy is 500,000 light-years wide and 20,000 light-years deep. Figuring that light travels at roughly 186,000 miles per second, it would take 500,000 light years just to travel from one side of our galaxy to the other. That's pretty significant commuting time. Also, there are approximately 150 billion stars in our galaxy, and scientists believe there are over a billion other galaxies. The God who created all of this is certainly capable of taking care of me!

Embarrassing as it is to admit, the way I respond to problems much of the time causes me to feel my faith in God is hypocritical. I find myself talking out of both sides of my mouth. Oh sure, I can deliver an inspirational message at a women's retreat about the power of God. But why is it so hard for me to translate this knowledge of God's greatness to the everyday grind of life? Do I really believe in a living God who created and sustains the universe, who demonstrated victory over death, *and* who says he cares immensely about me? How then can I forget so quickly he is bigger than any of my problems? I need to fess up that when my emotions feel out of control and I find myself thinking I'm not sure how much longer I can take this, I have lost sight of the incredible power of God and his promise to meet my needs. How can I need more than he chooses to provide for me at any given moment? I may be able to quote some pretty impressive statistics about him, but when I am filled with discontentment I reveal I really don't know him very well.

Not only do I need to focus on God's provision and his power, I need to remember who God says I am. I've never met a woman who prided herself in being selfish, cantankerous, and hard to live with. None of us wants her epitaph to read: "May she rest in peace; now we'll finally have some." As I thought one day about how I wanted my family and friends to describe me when I die, I wrote my own epitaph.

Here Lies Kathy Peel

Kathy Peel was the most incredible woman we've ever known. In everything she did, she pursued excellence and always delivered more than she promised. She was extremely disciplined and lived a life worth emulating. She brought God's beauty to everything she touched—whether a relationship, a room, or an event. She had a way of pushing people gently to do their best. She laughed a lot and brought joy to the lives of many.

When Bill read this he laughed hysterically. After I promised he'd be singing more than a few stanzas of "Can't Touch This" for the next week, he got the message I was really serious. Although it's lofty, and there are far more days than not when the epitaph I wrote sounds like someone else's, I read it regularly. I frequently fall on my face in defeat, making myself and everyone around me miserable.

During those fallen-down times, I must stop and ask, Who am I really? Am I as unlovely as I think? Am I a victim, powerless to do anything about my moods? Am I a failure? Am I really as empty as I feel?

What does God say about who I am? The Bible tells me, "If anyone is in Christ, he is a new creation" (2 Cor. 5:17). If I have Christ, I am a different person! When I became a Christian, I received a new identity. As a result, I have Christ's power, his potential, and his patience. I don't need to ask for these characteristics—I need to believe these things are true of me and act on this reality.

Oftentimes during that infamous time of the month, I feel anything but lovely. But God tells me that he loves me and accepts me as I am with all my flaws. "For I am convinced that nothing can ever separate us from his love. Death can't, and life can't. The angels won't, and all the powers of hell itself cannot keep God's love away. Our fears for today, our worries about tomorrow, or where we are—high above the sky, or in the deepest ocean—nothing will ever be able to separate us from the love of God demonstrated by our Lord Jesus Christ when he died for us" (Rom. 8:38–39 TLB). I am loved!

When I feel helpless to resist my volcanic vocabulary, I remind myself that God is able to do exceeding abundantly beyond all I ask or think, according to the power at work *within me* (Eph. 3:20). I can even control my tongue. I am powerful!

When my frequent failures smother me with guilt, I read, "Yes, all have sinned; all fall short of God's glorious ideal; yet now God declares us 'not guilty' of offending him if we trust in Jesus Christ, who in his kindness freely takes away our sins" (Rom. 3:23–24 TLB). I am forgiven!

When I feel empty and begin to focus on all the things I don't have, Ephesians 1:3 helps me remember that I have the unlimited treasure of heaven as my possession right now. "Praise be to the God and Father of our Lord Jesus Christ, who has blessed us in the heavenly realms with every spiritual blessing in Christ" (Eph. 1:3). I am rich!

This does not mean life is without pain and problems. It means I have the ability in Christ to rise above them. There are many days I feel like the Apostle Paul wrote about Jesus—he was "delivered over to death." But, as he says victoriously, "We are hard pressed on every side, but not crushed; perplexed, but not in despair; persecuted, but not abandoned; struck down, but not destroyed" (2 Cor. 4:8–9).

Although I have by no means "arrived" (as a matter of fact, I can't even see the station in the distance), I have learned how I see myself is critical. "As he thinketh in his heart so is he" (Prov. 23:7 KJV). If I think of myself as loved, I can love and accept others. If I see myself as forgiven, I can be gracious toward others. If I see myself as powerful, I can do what I know is right. If I see myself as full, I can give myself freely to others.

Early in our marriage Bill and I stumbled upon a poem that became our goal in dealing with daily struggles. After quoting this poem in a lecture at a conference, a dear woman made a beautiful cross-stitch of the verses and sent it to me. Although it hangs on the wall in our family room and serves as a daily reminder of where our focus should be, I still forget frequently. Only yesterday Bill had to remind me about "the theology of the doughnut." (I don't know who wrote this originally, but I first heard it from a college friend more than twenty years ago.)

As you travel through life my brother,
Whatever be your goal,
Keep your eye upon the doughnut,
And not upon the hole.

Daily concentrating on the positive side of life and remembering who I am in Christ is a difficult discipline. But I never want to quit trying. I'm convinced it could be the most important discipline I practice—for myself, my husband, and my children. I was personally inspired and reminded of this principle in the movie *Dances with Wolves*. John Dunbar arrived at his seemingly meaningless frontier post in the middle of nowhere only to find it in total disarray. Instead of letting the circumstances dictate his disposition, he focused on what he had. He saw himself as responsible and capable. Although no one was there to give him orders or to appreciate his work, he disciplined himself to work hard and make the most of the situation. He wrote in his journal, "I assigned myself the tasks of . . ." He refused to see himself as a victim, even though he was faced with insurmountable odds. That's the kind of person I want to be.

Daily Disciplines

"Would that every woman believed in the ideal of herself and hoped for it as the will of God"—George MacDonald.

Believing we can be our ideal selves doesn't necessarily mean we believe we're perfect. And falling short of our ideals doesn't mean we're failures and should quit trying. The wonderful thing about our God is that he gives us innumerable chances, on a daily basis, to be all we can be after we've failed in some way.

I've talked a lot about focus in this chapter, and about falling down and getting up again. Yet, if we don't know what we're getting up for or to—if we don't know ourselves well enough to know both our own shortcomings and our ideals—we'll never have anything to live up to.

Working daily disciplines is a good way to get to know ourselves and accept ourselves just as we are for now while we strive to meet our goals and ideals. It's also a very good way to figure out just exactly what our ideal of ourselves is.

Once again, I invite you to pick and choose among these expressions. Choose the ones that make the most sense for your life just now. Remember you can come back to others. And remember that trying to do everything at once almost certainly guarantees that you'll do nothing up to your ideal standards.

> ❦ Imagine that you are a butterfly in the corner of the ceiling looking down on yourself. What do you see?

> ❦ Do something active if you're feeling depressed. Take a walk. Do ten minutes of calisthenics. You gain energy by exerting energy.

> ❦ "I have learned to be content whatever the circumstances. I know what it is to be in need, and I know what it is to have plenty. I have learned the secret of being content in any and every situation, whether well fed or hungry,

whether living in plenty or in want" (Phil. 4:11b–12). The Apostle Paul wrote the letter to the Philippians from a jail cell. Do you ever feel like you're trapped in a cell? What does it look like? What plenty and contentment can you find in it?

❦ Take time out and let your senses communicate God's power and presence. When my emotions seem out of control, I try to experience God through his creation. Crushing autumn leaves under my feet, watching a sunrise, or picking flowers is refreshing to my spirit.

❦ Practice smiling at yourself in the mirror. You're uniquely beautiful.

❦ Hold your tongue. When your emotions feel out of control, don't allow yourself to say things you'll regret later.

❦ What are you feeling sorry for yourself about? I was inspired by a woman who was a guest on "The Home Show." Although she was paralyzed from the waist down and destined to spend the rest of her life in a wheelchair, she didn't feel sorry for herself. She began a special exercise program for handicapped people to keep the upper part of their bodies in shape and help others at the same time.

❦ Let yourself cry if you need to. Tears can be very cleansing.

❦ "I waited patiently for the Lord; he turned to me and heard my cry. He lifted me out of the slimy pit, out of the mud and mire; he set my feet on a rock and gave me a firm place to stand. He put a new song in my mouth, a hymn of praise to our God" (Psalm 40:1–3). Go ahead. It doesn't have to be great literature. Write your own hymn or psalm of praise to God in your life.

❦ Read *The Lost Princess* by George MacDonald. See if the princess reminds you of yourself sometimes.

❦ Get away alone to think and pray—even if it's just for a short time. Recently I felt the stresses in my life were almost too much to bear. I held my tears back until I dropped the kids off at school. I drove out into the country and cried for twenty minutes. Then I took myself out to breakfast and wrote my feelings in my prayer journal. I returned home with new strength.

❦ Don't let negative people determine your mood. Seek friends who inspire you.

❦ Instead of seeing your cup as half empty, try seeing it as half full.

❦ One thing we can always count on is change. If you're in the middle of a difficult situation, see it as a temporary stage in your life. Think about when it started. Remember now is not forever.

❦ Write your own epitaph. Read it regularly.

❦ Take time out daily to read part of a book that lifts your spirit.

❦ Make a list of everything you are thankful for. Don't forget to be thankful for things we often take for granted, such as two eyes, two hands, two feet, and a brain. If you're going through a particularly bad time, do this daily in your prayer journal. It doesn't have to be much, maybe only, "The house didn't burn down."

❦ Acknowledge and accept bad feelings. Don't bury them. I have a friend who says we must "own" our feelings before we can get rid of them. Sometimes it helps to talk about your feelings with a trusted friend. Or write down how you feel. Acknowledge your anger, sadness, grief. They may lead you to positive steps in living up to your ideal.

❦ Spend some time with a friend who makes you laugh. I have two close friends who live in different cities. We try to get together three or four times a year just to laugh together.

❦ Volunteer your time and talents at a soup kitchen, hospital, or shelter for the homeless. Focus your thoughts on helping others.

❦ Open your windows and let as much light as possible come into your house. Darkness can be depressing. If you don't have a nice view, put a pretty window box full of colorful flowers outside your window.

❦ Display things around your home or work environment that bring fond memories to mind. I keep my thirty-year-old Chatty Cathy doll in our bedroom. It makes me smile when I think about playing house as a young girl. I also enjoy keeping postcards and notes from close friends above my desk. When I reread them, I am blessed.

❦ Look your best for yourself. Getting into the rut of being sloppy in your appearance can drag you down. If I find myself sinking into a negative mood, I take a fragrant bubble bath, wash and style my hair, and put on a pretty outfit. It makes me feel better when I like what I see in the mirror.

❦ Avoid overwork and burnout. Schedule regular times to play.

❦ Give yourself the freedom to do something you've always wanted to do . . . just for fun. At age thirty-seven I began piano lessons again after a sixteen-year layoff.

❦ Be wise in your personal habits if you're experiencing PMS. Exercise as much as possible, get plenty of rest, don't eat sweets, and cut back on caffeine.

❦ Keep an "emotion" calendar for a month or two. This can help you pinpoint when you're dealing with PMS and other mood swings. It can also help you remember now is not forever.

❦ Write down all of your feelings in a letter to God. He cares.

❦ Read biographies of people who have overcome big obstacles in their lives such as Helen Keller, Wilma Rudolf, and Abraham Lincoln.

❦ "The kingdom of God is within you" (Luke 17:21). Pray quietly every day that you'll find and recognize it when you see it.

❦ Whether at work or at home, focus on positive things at mealtime. The brain creates body chemicals that counteract effective digestion when we worry, fret, argue, or process negative thoughts.

❦ Listen to an inspiring book on cassette tape. If you don't feel like reading, this is a great way to focus your thoughts on something positive and helpful.

❦ "Always take an emergency leisurely"—Chinese Proverb. Make this your daily motto.

❦ Get busy and do what you can to make your world better.

Self-Disciplines

❦ "If you have to move one inch from where you are right now to be happy, you never will be"—Tim Hansel. What does this mean to you? If you feel you could never be happy in your present situation, try writing a letter to God and expressing your feelings, no matter how discontent or negative you feel. David did this in the Psalms. Just seeing your circumstances written down can help you gain a new perspective and sometimes can give you creative ideas about your situation.

3

You're Smarter Than You Look: Keeping Up the Image

*W*hen Bill and I announced our engagement, his fraternity brothers couldn't believe he was marrying the campus airhead. I can't imagine what gave them that idea. Actually, I took college life very seriously. To me, a formal education was measured by how many party dresses I had in my closet. Physical science meant studying the body structure of the offensive line of the football team. Chemistry was something that happened when I met a cute guy. And Spanish was necessary for shopping across the border. On a campus crawling with prelaw, premedical, and preseminary students, the only thing I thought about was Where's the pre-party?

I was no goof-off, mind you. I always got up for my eleven o'clock class. And I never missed my three-hour biology lab on rainy days. (On sunny days I studied algae by the pool.)

A certain freedom of spirit dominated not only my lifestyle but the entire culture of the late 1960s. Doing your own thing was the philosophy of the day. Not wanting to live a double standard, I applied this line of thinking to courses that cramped my style. I simply did my own thing: I dropped them. My parents never figured out the mystery of the college grading system—why they paid tuition for fifteen semester hours, but only received grades for six.

To say the least, my lifestyle was a bit disconcerting to my 4.0 roommate. "It's time for you to settle down and get serious about studying—not to mention life," she suggested firmly. "I'm setting you up with a guy whose head is screwed on right. He's an old high-school friend who's intelligent, spiritual, and responsible. You never know—maybe you'll like him. And his study habits might even rub off on you. Stranger things have happened."

That blind date was a pivotal point in my intellectual growth, as well as other indicators of my maturity level. Since Bill was on academic scholarship, he studied a lot. If I wanted to see him, I had to meet him on his turf—the library, formerly foreign territory to me. So I did what everyone else in the library did . . . I studied. To my surprise, I discovered the more I studied, the more I learned. And the more I learned, the more I enjoyed learning. I became an avid reader with an unquenchable thirst never to stop learning.

Bill and I spent so many wonderful hours in the library. We had great fun discussing what we learned, and as a result, grew closer. I decided then I wanted to spend the rest of my life with a man I could talk to. And I wanted to have something to talk about. So I vowed to keep learning.

I read the classic books I was supposed to have studied in high school and college. To that point, I'd only read the Cliff Notes. After graduating from college, I took one class each semester, sat on the front row, and took copious notes. I couldn't get enough. Although I looked like a dumb blonde, I was determined not to be one. I continued my newly found academic adventure . . . that is, until we had children.

During the diaper dispensation of our lives I found it difficult to schedule time for improving my brain power. But I was not totally without intellectual stimulation. I used sophisticated problem-solving techniques every day. I used deductive reasoning to figure out how to remove gummy bears that had taken root and were now growing in the carpet. I was first to discover that the apple juice left in a bottle under the sofa for two weeks makes a nice salad vinegar. And how to scoop a bowel movement from my one-year-old's bath water was always a real brain teaser. Small wonder my IQ dropped below my shoe size.

As the kids grew older I grabbed moments any time I could to read and study. Just about the time I started feeling good about myself intellectually again, we had teenagers. Although it's a universal axiom that all teenagers think their parents are stupid, I didn't want to believe it. I boasted (in a moment of delirium) that ours would not be typical teenagers. I predicted they would reverently come before us and say, "Mom and Dad, we are privileged to have parents so intellectually astute, culturally upbeat, emotionally solid, and spiritually sound. Surely we are more blessed than all other children."

No, our kids would look at us as one of them, not as the older generation. They would automatically accept our values, appreciate our tastes, and model our lifestyle. Hungering to know what we've learned from the experience of age, they would hang on our every word.

Yes, I have an extensive fantasy life.

Actually, it's a miracle we can communicate at all without an interpreter. I learned that to carry on a semi-intelligent discussion with a teenager, I had to be bilingual, with English as my *second* language. I've always thought a *Teenage Dictionary of Current Terms* would be a big money-maker. But it would have to be updated monthly. Maybe a magazine. Or possibly a cassette tape I could learn from during drive time. Then I'd understand my seventeen-year-old when he meets me at the door and says: "Yo, Mom. Later please? Homecoming's Friday, and it's a hate. I'm taking Kim. She's fine, but a real hoser. I love my coat—NOT! It's nappy. I feel totally cheese ball. There's a bad coat I want. If I treed and found it on sale, could you spring by Friday? I have a lot of cash you know. Psych!"

I would know he means, "Hi Mom. I expected you to be home earlier. I have a date to homecoming even though I dislike dances. I'm taking Kim. She's cute but acts a little dumb sometimes. My coat is looking a little dated. Actually it's tacky and I feel completely out of style. I've found one I really like. If I get lucky and find it on sale, could you buy it before Friday? I don't have any money."

Although we've picked up a few basic communication skills, our age and experience mean nothing. Often they work against us. Just last week our kids reminded us what they thought about our generation. Bill and I walked through the family room on the way out the door to a "Back to Woodstock" party. We thought our costumes were so hip—bell-bottoms, tie-dyed shirts, peace symbols, psychedelic hair, and headbands. "We won't stay long at the party guys," I said as they stared in unbelief.

"You're not going out in public—please say you're not," Joel broke the silence.

"Dad, lose the beard. Your Led Zeppelin look doesn't work, *at all*," John pleaded with embarrassment. "I can't believe your generation was so *stupid*. Woodstock, Timothy Leary, Jimi Hendrix . . . give me a break. You couldn't possibly have learned anything in college. You were too busy going to sit-ins."

Since they're suspicious of the intellectual acumen of anyone our age, I know they're really desperate when they ask for help with homework. They seem shocked when we happen to remember anything about dominant and recessive genes or the battle of Gettysburg.

As we all know, a seventeen-year-old is smarter than anyone within a fifty-mile radius. Ours thinks one of his God-given duties in life is to inform his less-knowledgeable younger brothers about the hazards of living with an aging, mentally deficient mother. The ways he sees it, why tell Aggie jokes when we've got Mom around? He taught them to personalize a few of the latest blonde jokes just for me.

"Want to know how you can tell when Mom's been using her computer?" John astutely asked Joel and James. "There's whiteout on the screen."

After recovering from hysteria Joel chimed in, "Do you know how to make Mom's eyes sparkle?"

"How?" James asked.

"Shine a flashlight in her ears."

"I love it!" John responded as he caught his breath. "Hey, have you ever wondered if all that mousse Mom uses on her hair is seeping into her brain causing premature senility?"

On that one I burst through the swinging door I'd been hiding behind and snapped, "Okay you guys, read my lips. You're all going to boarding school!"

"Promise?" they answered in unison.

"You think you're funny don't you?" I retorted. "Let's see if you laugh when I get my next royalty check and don't spend any of it on you!"

"Well," I thought to myself as I walked out of the room, "I know the kids are teasing, but I don't want to wake up one morning and discover I have put my brain in neutral and it won't go back in gear." So despite the fact that their teasing keeps me on my toes, it also is a daily reminder that I want to keep up with life. I want to be able to talk with them—and with Bill—about what they're interested in. But, more importantly, I want to use my brain to stretch and grow the way I think God intended me to.

Luke 2:52 says that Jesus grew in four ways: in wisdom (intellectually), in stature (physically), in the knowledge of God (spiritually), and in favor with man (socially and emotionally). Many times we tend to think that God is only interested in our spiritual growth, when the truth of the matter is he wants us to live a fully rounded life. He is equally interested in our growth in the other areas of our life as well—which includes the intellectual. This doesn't happen automatically.

A woman in her fifties told me the sad story of how she awoke one day and realized the emptiness of her intellectual life. When her children were young her life revolved totally around them. The only escapes she enjoyed were daily soap operas and a weekly bridge club. Her literary pursuits were limited to sale advertisements, catalogs, and romance novels. When her husband came home at night, their communication consisted of how the children were wearing on her nerves, what appliance needed fixing, and which stores were having sales. Her husband's business caused him to stay on the cutting edge of new thoughts and trends. When they reached the empty-nest stage of life, they could hardly carry on a conversation. She regretted not striving to be an interesting person for herself and for him. In the end, she didn't enjoy her own company, and he found someone else younger and more stimulating.

This story left me shaking in my boots. Then a trip to the beauty salon deepened my apprehension. It also put the fear of God in me about keeping my mind not only in gear, but moving in a productive direction. I overheard a conversation between two sixty-something women. While getting her hair dyed an interesting shade of purple, one talked about her doctors, the latest flavors of laxatives, and what Vanna White wore on television last night. The other responded with the latest gossip concerning everyone in her family, neighborhood, and Sunday school class. I don't want to be critical, but I hope my golden years will be a little more intellectually stimulating.

So I made a resolution to apply Samuel Johnson's quote: "The future is purchased by the present." I knew if I wanted to be an interesting person to myself, to Bill and to others, then I had a lot of work to do.

It didn't come to me overnight how I might do this. But I knew I wanted to, for the future, yes, but also for the benefit of my daily life. My kids were little and there were times when I was desperate for adult company— especially my own adult company. I felt like a voice crying out from a wilderness of diapers, wooden blocks, and ABC books. When do I get to do something that stimulates my mind, dear God?

And as he usually does, God answered my desperate cry. I began to see that one thing I had to do was to spend time with people other than small children— people who would force me to think about something other than peanut butter sandwiches. Isolation is no friend to mental development. So I looked for sharp intellectual people, carved time out of my schedule to spend time with them, and picked their brains. I learned priceless information about business, history, literature, plus a vast array of other topics. I am continually amazed at what other people know and are willing to share if I ask.

I also figured out that staying involved with other people's needs helped me as much as it helped them. When I am wrapped up with myself, I make a very small package. So I organized a neighborhood study and support group. We were all young moms, busy with diaper changing, car pooling, and pediatrician appointments.

The time we spent together studying the Bible and other books, sharing our struggles, and meeting each other's needs was stimulating as well as therapeutic. Our group grew as we invited friends from other neighborhoods to join. Since we had diverse backgrounds, interests, and educations, we learned a lot from each other. Today, fifteen years later, we are still close friends although many of us now live in different cities.

Early on in the process of growing intellectually, I discovered that I wouldn't grow if I didn't allow myself to be curious. No matter what the subject or pursuit, I need to give myself the freedom to take time to study it. Sad but true, I came in contact with a group of Christians who believed the only thing worth studying is the Bible. Anything else is worldly. It was so freeing to realize that no matter what I study—whether biology, English literature, business, mathematics, or art history—God is in the midst of it. All truth is his truth. God gave me a mind, and I am sure he meant for me to use it. A faith that requires me to put my mind on the shelf is not the faith of the Bible. God wants me to wrestle intellectually with knotty problems so that I can form convictions rather than be driven by unthought-through prejudices. Sure, there are some wacky thoughts and published ideas out there. But mature, intellectually fit Christians can distinguish between truth and fantasy.

Besides being curious, I need to give myself the freedom to explore and look into a variety of interests. There were days in my early thirties when I thought I might never do anything but muck around with finger paints and clay. I found when I allowed myself to participate in diverse adult interests, I could enjoy rather than endure playing childish games with my kids.

When I set out to do all this, I found myself pursuing some things I thought I would like, but didn't. I started some classes and didn't finish them—or finished them without a sense of satisfaction. But if I hadn't explored those things, I wouldn't have discovered others, including knowing a whole lot more about what I do and think.

Taking advantage of lectures or seminars offered in my community is a good way to explore new interests. It's quite inexpensive and requires a minimum time commitment at first. I also enrolled in classes (one per semester) at a local university and even took a correspondence course. You may want to consider finishing a degree you started years before or pursuing a postgraduate degree. There are also educational programs offered on public television. Taking courses or attending seminars and lectures helps put new learning in context, introduces us to new people as well as new ideas, and keeps us stimulated.

Plus, committing to a course helps me be tenacious. I knew when I found something I enjoyed learning about I would have to fight for the time to pursue this interest. It takes discipline to work my schedule to take a class or read a book on a particular subject. Sometimes I have to get up earlier or stay up later to learn something new.

If I wanted to learn new things, I knew I couldn't hold on to the attitude I don't have time to learn something new. I'm too busy meeting everyone else's needs. I knew this was an excuse. If I really wanted to pursue a personal endeavor, I could choose to do it. Besides, when I do learn new things and meet my own needs for intellectual stimulation, I come back to meeting other people's needs more refreshed and often with new ideas. Many young mothers who were ready to throw up their hands in despair have benefited from taking child psychology or parenting classes with others in the same situation.

Now saying I'm going to make time for myself is one thing. And doing it is quite another. I learned that if I waited until I had big blocks of time to start something new I'd never do it. So I learned how to seize the day or the hour or the minute. I stopped watching television unless I had a purpose for watching the program. I realized useless television was robbing me of moments I could be learning something new.

I began to use time I spent doing mundane activities as "think" time. Einstein claimed he got all his best ideas while shaving. I get many of my good ideas listening to Mozart or other good music while driving on the freeway.

Seizing opportunities meant I began grabbing moments that otherwise would have been wasted. I take a book with me on appointments when I even suspect I might have to wait. I try to keep a book in the car so I'll have it if I have to wait unexpectedly. I also listen to books on cassettes during errand time. Do you know the average person spends twenty-seven hours a year sitting at traffic lights? If you commute by public transportation, you probably have hours of time a week when you could be reading or thinking.

It's certainly not always easy to find time for learning. I've found I have to be willing to work hard. To have time for personal pursuits means I have to use my time wisely and work hard to get my other responsibilities finished.

When I started my daily discipline of improving my mind and expanding my horizons any way I could, I began to collect odd bits of information. I made a list of topics that interested me and began collecting articles, statistics, and quotes on these subjects. Little did I know that this information would be part of my books some day. (How do you think I knew the average amount of time people spend sitting at stoplights?)

Over the years, as I developed my daily intellectual disciplines, I've searched for older people to emulate in this area. I've found a few people to be role models.

I loved Doris the moment I met her at a women's conference. Dressed in a colorful warmup suit and tennis shoes, she had just finished a brisk walk. When she smiled, her entire face lit up as each line enhanced her countenance. As we talked I learned that she reads two books a month and takes each of her grandchildren on an educational trip once a year. Last year when she learned to parasail, her only fear was losing her dentures over the ocean. At age seventy-five she lives each day to the fullest.

Then there's Eleanor, a seventy-six-year-young friend whose schedule is busier than mine. A widow for thirty-one years, she has given her life to counseling and teaching the Bible. She reads and studies regularly, and daily keeps up with world events. She travels extensively on speaking engagements, and once a month drives five hours to Washington, D.C. to teach congressional and military wives. She is intellectually sharp, physically beautiful, emotionally stable, and spiritually in tune. When I asked her secret, she said she is so busy doing what she feels God has called her to do and so involved in the lives of others, she doesn't have a choice but to stay as sharp as possible.

And my own parents set a good example of staying active and having fun. When I called home one Saturday morning at 10:00, I was a little concerned they were just getting out of bed. But when I learned they had been dancing until 1:00 A.M., then played cards with friends (in their mid-eighties) until 4:00 A.M., I was glad they'd slept late. Daddy still performed his morning reading routine, although he started a little later than usual.

A friend who practices medicine told me chronological age sometimes has very little to do with how old a person is. His patients in their nineties are often "younger" than patients in their sixties because of their attitudes. The "young ones" all have three things in common: a sense of purpose for their lives; a commitment to concentrate on what's right instead of what's wrong; and an environment full of outside interests and people that keep them intellectually stimulated.

The sad truth is that as many people grow older, they not only lack a sense of purpose, concentrate on their problems, and focus on themselves, but they act as though the shelf life of their brain has expired. They also buy into a personal survival mentality. Eileen Guder states the case well in *God, But I'm Bored:*

> You can live on bland food so as to avoid an ulcer; drink no tea or coffee or other stimulants, in the name of health; go to bed early and stay away from night life; avoid all controversial subjects so as never to give offense; mind your own business and avoid involvement in other people's problems, spend money only on necessities, and save all you can. You can still break your neck in the bathtub, and it will serve you right.

I'm beginning to see there's an art to growing intellectually while at the same time growing old. I'm convinced we won't automatically become interesting, vivacious senior citizens the day our first Social Security check arrives. A philosophy of making our days count, rather than merely surviving and counting our days starts now—wherever we are. How we spend time in our thirties, forties, and fifties will determine what we'll be like in our sixties, seventies, and eighties. But sometimes it's hard to remember this when you have a baby pulling at your hemline, a grade-schooler participating in every activity available, a teenager fighting peer pressure, and a husband needing feminine attention. I have to keep reminding myself that I am worthless to those I love if I don't take time to develop myself.

Over the years, I've come up with these guidelines. If they speak to you, I suggest you write them out and post them somewhere you can see them. They'll remind you that improving our brains a little bit at a time, day after day, can lead to feeling less desperate now and pave the way for a more interesting future.

Keep-on-Growing Guidelines

1. Set a goal to study a new subject and learn something new each year.
2. Allow myself to be curious.
3. Give myself the freedom to fail.
4. Be jealous of my time and use it well.
5. Collect information even if I don't know how I'm going to use it.
6. Focus on the long-term benefits.

Five minutes a day spent growing intellectually may not seem like much, but that adds up to over thirty hours a year of personal "class time."

Daily Disciplines

"The desirableness of a life is to be measured by the amount of interest and not the amount of ease in it, for the more ease, the more unrest"—George MacDonald.

An interesting life is not necessarily an easy life. And God never promised us an easy life. What he did promise is to be there for us. And when we go to him with our problems, I think one of the things he gives us is the challenge of learning something new. That's what makes life interesting. Too much ease in life leads us to be bored and complacent. Life passes us by, and we run the risk of living death—of being disconnected from those we love, living a dull life, and enduring a boring old age.

George MacDonald's quote has this wisdom in it: We may think it's ease we want. But ease leads, easily and often, to unrest. When we work to make our lives interesting we'll still have problems. But we'll have the resources to deal with them.

Once again, the disciplines listed in this Daily Disciplines section are here for you to pick and choose from. Some of them can be done daily—like reading and praying. Some are to be done weekly, once-a-month, or less frequently. Choose those that appeal to you. Come back to this chapter when you're feeling like your life is boring. Find something new to do or learn.

- ❦ "You don't grow old. You get old by not growing"—E. Stanley Jones. What can you do today to grow intellectually?

- ❦ Education helps us live a more quality life by continually stretching our minds. Enroll in a class at a community college or take a correspondence course.

- ❦ When you find an author who stimulates you, try to read everything he or she has written.

- ❦ Pray daily that God will help you maximize your intellectual potential and allow you to use what you learn for his purposes.

- ❦ Set aside time to talk with your husband about politics, books, current events, etc.—not the kids, the roof, or the dog.

- ❦ Buy a good dictionary, keep it close at hand, and use it. Try to learn one new vocabulary word each week. (A word-a-day calendar is an easy way to do this.)

❦ When you're studying a particular subject, try to see God in what you're studying. Take time out to pray and thank him for creating the universe. We can see his hand in the pages of history. We study science and math because he is the author. We enjoy architecture and interior design because he created colors, shapes, textures, and our ability to see, feel, and enjoy them.

❦ Write facts you want to remember or interesting quotes in a notebook or on index cards. Categorize and file them for future reference.

❦ Check out how-to videos from the library on a subject you've always wanted to know more about.

❦ Don't let age be a barrier to your dreams. At age eighty-one Thomas Edison patented his last invention. In his seventies Frank Lloyd Wright designed many of his masterpieces.

❦ Start a book club. Invite friends to read the same book, then get together once a month to discuss what you read.

❦ Keep paper and pens by your bed in case you get a brainstorm in the middle of the night.

❦ Read a book with your husband. Analyze what you learn together.

❦ You're only young once, but you can be young at heart forever. Are you feeling depressed because you're getting older? Ask yourself, What have I always wanted to do? Give yourself the freedom to do it!

❦ Ask God to help you learn something new, study for a test, or remember important facts. He created your mind and cares that you use it.

❧ Find an older mentor to learn from. Dr. Cecelia Hurwich, a psychologist in Berkeley, California, studied vivacious women in their seventies. She found the women who lived life in the present, squeezing from daily life all its vitality and viewing the world with a positive eye, each had a mentor who influenced her life.

❧ Close your eyes and picture what you'll be like twenty years from now. Do you like what you see? What discipline will you begin today so you'll be the best you can be tomorrow?

❧ "It is only the ignorant who despise education"—Publilius Syrus. What does this mean to you?

❧ Always keep at least one good book going. Remember, we are influenced by what we select. I read three or four at the same time. My mood decides which one I read that day. If you read one book each month you're in the top 1 percent of the intellectuals in America.

❧ Strive to be a stimulating conversationalist about interesting topics and principles. If you're not growing intellectually, this will affect your self-image. It is then easy to digress into talking about people. Remember, a gossip is a "leveler" . . . "If I can't get up to her level, I'll pull her down to mine by spreading gossip."

❧ Attend a lecture with a friend who stimulates you. Talk about what you learned.

❧ Create an environment conducive to learning. Surround yourself with good books, play stimulating music, keep your desk supplied with study supplies, and turn off the television.

🐝 "Iron sharpens iron, so one man sharpens another" (Prov. 27:17). Be accountable to a motivational friend if you need a mental energy boost. I have a good friend who regularly asks me what I'm reading and learning.

🐝 Organize a trip to take with friends who push you to be your best. You'll feel invigorated and refreshed when you return.

🐝 Don't be afraid to go back to school. You'll be surprised at how much you remember. I was shocked when I passed the GRE at age thirty-seven.

🐝 Fill your life with new experiences. Last year I decided to try to understand more of Shakespeare's writings, conquer a new computer program, and learn to roller blade.

🐝 "Reading is to the mind what exercise is to the body"—Sir Richard Steele. What other analogies come to your mind about learning, thinking, and praying? How will you keep the muscles of your mind fit?

🐝 Make a commitment never to stop learning.

Self-Disciplines

🐝 Start a list of things you're interested in. It's great to have such a list when you're feeling bored. And it's hard to think of new things when life seems disinteresting.

4
Working Girl

In my mid-thirties I dreamed of becoming president of my own company. In my fantasy, surrounded by a helpful staff, I had a quaint corner office with a great view and antique cherry furniture. I wore expensive linen suits, silk blouses, and large tortoise-shell glasses (kind of a Wall Street look). I juggled appointments to fit *Inc.* magazine into my schedule for a cover photo. And Peter Drucker stopped by regularly for coffee. In my mind, I did business in a world where banks never called in loans, contracts never needed negotiating, and the IRS didn't care if you kept records. But alas, my fantasy business became real one day. And you guessed it, it wasn't exactly what I expected.

Dressed in my leotard and aerobic-dance shoes, I balanced the telephone receiver between my shoulder and ear. I tried to carry on a halfway intelligent conversation with the editor of a major business magazine on the other end while I wiped peanut butter from James's face and tied his shoes. I hoped the editor couldn't hear the dog barking and the perma-press dryer buzzer in the background. "As president of Creative People, Inc. you must stay very busy writing, speaking, and developing new products," he commented. "I understand you've sold over 500,000 books. What does it feel like to be a successful professional woman?"

Thankful I didn't have a video telephone, I answered in my most professional voice: "I feel quite fulfilled in my work. I have the privilege of performing an assortment of tasks, working with a variety of people, and spending time daily in different places." Not wanting to shatter his corporate image of me, I decided not to tell him my assortment of tasks includes washing, cooking, and car pooling, as well as writing books and running a company. Or that I deal with not only editors, heads of corporations, and media personnel, but first graders, middle schoolers, and high schoolers as well. And my daily travels take me from my desk piled with business, school, and family papers in the living room to my computer in the master bedroom where I write to the washer to throw in a load of blue jeans. I take advantage of the dryer time to make duplicates of documents on my copy machine in the utility room. Then I run to the fax machine in another bedroom to send the documents. Trump Tower it's not.

There are plenty of days when I feel stretched to the limit answering phone calls and faxes, meeting deadlines, and trying to finish my work by 3:00 so I can pick up the kids and get them to their various practices and meetings. But I love my work and crazy working conditions—except for the hazards of traveling.

Sometimes I amaze myself. I have an uncanny ability to get into desperate situations, especially on business trips. Here's a case in point. After a full day of book promoting, I finished my last television spot in Denver. As I hurriedly packed my autumn dog-and-pony show for my coauthored book, *A Mother's Manual for Holiday Survival,* it crossed my mind that I resembled part of the road crew from Ringling Brothers' Circus. I thought about professional women who travel with a lap-top computer and leather briefcase. Instead of a portfolio of important papers, I travel with five bags full of fall squash candle holders, a new-potato wreath, decorated pumpkins, hurricane lantern, pomegranates, fall leaves, pine cones, and pilgrim hats filled with popcorn and candy corn. I lugged my bags to the rental car knowing I'd best get to the airport fast or else I'd miss my plane.

I climbed into the unfamiliar car and found the windshield wipers, radio, defroster, air conditioner, hazard light, and hood release before finally locating the headlights. When I turned the ignition key, the seat belt closed around me like an Indiana Jones booby trap. (I have a few choice words for the idiot in Detroit who invented those belts.) I hate being at the mercy of a high-tech car. To make matters worse, I didn't have a clue as to how to get to the airport, and I only had forty-five minutes to get there.

About that time a Federal Express truck pulled up in front of me. Ah . . . who else would better know the streets of Denver, I thought. *I'll use the old damsel-in-distress approach.* After a five-second hair fluff, lipstick touch-up, and squirt of perfume, I made my move. As the car withdrew its tentacles, I jumped out and approached the driver. "Excuse me sir," I used my most helpless feminine voice, "I wonder if you could tell me how to get to the airport?"

Unimpressed with my charm, he hardly glanced up, then answered in one breath, "SureTakeEleventheastto BroadwaythengonorthtwoblockstoColfaxtoUniversity theneastonMLKandfollowthesigns . . . you can't miss it." He jumped in his truck and sped off to make his next delivery deadline.

"Okay, Kathy, you have a college degree," I said to myself. "No problemo." I took off.

After traveling eight blocks, the reality of my situation hit. Trust me, you don't know fear until you've been in a strange city after dark, driving a rental car during rush-hour traffic in a snowstorm, only to find yourself in the adult-only district of downtown not knowing whether you're getting closer to the airport or farther from it. To my left I saw a line of people standing in the snow waiting for the doors to open for the female mud wrestling match between Daring DeeDee and Tantalizing Tanya. And the theater marquee on my right read "The Escapades of Luscious Lolita." I envisioned the following morning's headline: BUDDING AUTHORESS RAPED OUTSIDE X-RATED PEEP SHOW AFTER WRECKING RENTAL CAR: INVESTIGATORS UNABLE TO EXPLAIN TENTACLE MARKS ACROSS HER CHEST.

Spotting a policeman two lanes over, I dodged a patch of ice and two lanes of traffic to chase him down. I pulled in front of his patrol car and stopped at a red light. Wondering what moving violation I could commit, I thought, What have I got to lose? A jail cell would be safer than where I am right now. I leapt from my car and ran back to the police car and asked for directions. He spurted out a few highway numbers then pointed at the green light to remind me I was holding up fifty cars. I ran back to my car, jumped in, and sped off. Involuntarily I took the scenic route and arrived at the airport three minutes before my plane was scheduled to take off—only to learn it had been delayed. Thanks to the snowstorm in Denver and tornadoes in Dallas, I could now sit down and have a coronary at leisure.

Realizing my bladder had reached its limit in diet cola, I proceeded to look for the airport restroom—a place I avoid unless absolutely desperate. Airport restrooms are an enigma to me—especially ones that have toilets that flush automatically. I've always wanted to fool the little magic eye that supposedly knows when I'm through. Just thinking about it makes me crazy. I've tried covering it with my hand and squatting low enough to get under its beam. I've even attempted a sidesaddle approach. It always knows when to flush—which makes me think there's someone behind the wall watching.

Then I walked the length of the terminal three times trying to drop a few inches from my heavily endowed hips. I also read the covers of every magazine on the newsstand. Finally I saw the gate agent point out the window and yell, "De plane! De plane!" I prepared to board.

I would be remiss at this point if I didn't share my deepest feelings about flying: It stinks. After experiencing more than my share of planes dropping a few thousand feet in midair, hitting thunderstorms that cause dinner to land in the aisle, and engines overheating at thirty-three thousand feet, I've decided I don't like being anyplace higher than I can jump from and land comfortably. But since my career dictates that I travel two to three times a month, I've been forced to create a number of defense mechanisms to deal with my fear of flying. I have been known to rip shirt sleeves off of businessmen seated next to me, leave fingernail clawmarks in the vinyl armrests, and make a complete fool of myself trying to find someone in the cabin who will listen to me talk nonstop through the flight so I forget I'm in the air. I didn't figure out until we landed that a lady who listened to me all the way from Dallas to Kansas City once didn't speak a word of English. (I thought she was totally enraptured with my life story since she nodded and smiled for an hour and a half.)

On this particular snowy night I sat alone. As I recapped my day, I thought about how, in spite of flying, I really do love my work. Writing, speaking, being a guest on hundreds of television and radio shows, working with fun and stimulating people—what a privilege!

I closed my eyes and reminisced about how it all started. It was a beautiful autumn morning in East Texas. We were at an old restored inn with other couples for a retreat. Bill was the speaker, and his messages dealt with getting in touch with what God wants to do with your life. Trying to look like an attentive wife—hanging on my husband's every word—I was really thinking, I'm sure I've heard this before. I'll secretly work on my "to do" list for next week. I tried to tune him out.

But something Bill said struck a responsive chord within me. He captured my attention when he read Psalm 37:4: "Delight yourself in the Lord and he will give you the desires of your heart." After asking the group to write down ten desires that we've always wanted to do, Bill instructed us to not let anything limit our dreams—not education, finances, location, age, or any kind of circumstances. We were to just permit ourselves to think about what we would really like to do if there were nothing holding us back.

We went our separate ways to find a quiet place to think, not only about our specific desires, but whether or not we truly believed what God said in this Psalm—that if we delight ourselves in him, he will place his desires within our hearts.

I made my list, but I was embarrassed to share it openly because my dreams seemed so lofty. I laughed aloud at myself when I read the first three items on my list. My first dream was to write a book. "How in the Sam Hill," I reprimanded myself, "could you be so presumptuous to think you could write a book? But yet, my assignment is to get in touch with my desires, and writing is something I've always wanted to do." I daydreamed for a moment and traveled back twenty-five years to the clubhouse I built in my backyard. It was there that I created and wrote a neighborhood newspaper. I used my daddy's carbon paper to make copies of my newspaper that I sold for a nickel each.

I also remembered that over the years I gravitated toward the writing jobs within clubs and organizations. I even produced a newsletter that I sent to five hundred women. "Yes," I confirmed, "I do have a deep desire to write. And if I ever have the privilege, I would like to write about helping women become all God created them to be . . . as individuals, wives, mothers, and professionals." I got goose bumps just thinking about it!

The second desire I wrote was to speak to large groups of women. I fantasized about standing on a stage in front of the five hundred women to whom I had written. I could feel the excitement of causing them to laugh, listen, and learn God's truths. "Oh, what an incredible privilege that would be! But it's all right, Lord, if I never get to do that," I prayed in unbelief. "I'm probably not good enough. But just keep me in your speaker file if you ever need someone to fill a spot."

Next on my list was to pass the Graduate Record Examination and get a master's degree in journalism and communications. This desire caused me to think I was not playing with a full deck. I scoffed, "Get real, Peel! You really think you can pass the GRE and be accepted into graduate school? Just how many quadratic equations have you worked lately?"

Six weeks passed, and I couldn't get my list of desires off my mind. I decided to step out and do what was within my power to make some of these dreams come to pass. I asked God to do his part if he wanted them to happen. I prayed that he would open doors for me to speak. I also signed up to take the GRE and enrolled in the postgraduate program at the University of Texas.

Then I decided to write a book. But I had one small problem. I had to think of something to write about. About that time my oldest son John approached me and put his arm around my shoulder. He said, "Mom, no offense, but . . . you don't cook very well, and you can't sew, and you're sure not a very good housekeeper, but at least we have a good time around our house."

So how was I supposed to respond to a comment like that? I decided I could either throw myself across the bed and sob over the fact that I'm a domestic failure, or I could focus on something I do fairly well—make our home a fun place to be. I chose the latter, and it occurred to me that maybe, just maybe, God could use me to help other moms create a wonderful atmosphere in their homes.

I approached Bill with his usual Saturday "Honey-do" list, only this time I added a little something extra. I asked him to fix the front door. clean out the garage, caulk the tub, and publish a book. "Publish a book!" he exclaimed. "What do you mean publish a book?"

"Now look," I firmly replied, "you got me into this! I'm just following your advice and getting in touch with the desires within my heart." Knowing he couldn't deny it, he acquiesced and said, "Okay, but please try not to lose too much money."

It was the first of January when I started thinking about what felt needs all moms have in common. *Summer!* I thought. Every mother in America pulls her hair out during the summer. This would be a great time to start creating a fun, family atmosphere. Excitedly I called a friend, Joy Mahaffey, who had taught a summertime seminar for moms at our church. "Joy, we're going to write a book, and Bill is going to publish it for us!"

The next three months flew by. Writing, editing, choosing type style, laying out the pages, deciding on interior art, paper, and binding, finding cover art—we learned a lot fast. The first copies of *A Mother's Manual for Summer Survival* rolled off the press March 31, 1988.

Thrilled to have the actual product in hand, I hopped in my car and drove to Dallas. (The highway patrol might suggest I use the word "flew" to Dallas.) I stopped at the city limits, found a pay phone, and looked up "Bookstores" in the yellow pages. I chose the six best advertisements and headed for those stores.

Trying to look as calm and professional as possible (it was a struggle), I walked into each store and said, "Hi! I'm Kathy Peel and this is *A Mother's Manual for Summer Survival*. I think every mom who walks into your store will buy this book. How many would you like to order?"

Well, shock of my life, they all bought the book! This was too good to be true. Realizing this little project might just be bigger than we anticipated, I drove back to Tyler in a twilight-zone state. When I returned home, we sat around the kitchen table and wrote a homespun marketing plan. Shortly afterwards, we began to receive orders regularly. After only nine weeks we sold 15,000 copies.

I decided we needed some national exposure, but we had no money for advertising. So I mailed our overnight success story and a copy of the book to the major networks. Amazingly, CNN picked it up. This was more exciting than we could possibly imagine. On a warm day in early June the CNN van pulled up in front of my average American home where seventeen children were bouncing off the walls waiting to be on international television. The reporter and cameraman had just flown in from the demilitarized zone in Panama where the cameraman had been shot. I could tell by the look on their faces they wondered why on earth they were in Tyler, Texas, doing a stupid story about two East Texas housewives and some book they wrote. Frankly, I didn't care what they thought. I was just glad they were there.

After our story was featured five times within a twenty-four hour period on CNN, we began to receive phone calls from mothers all across America and five foreign countries. The word "distribution" took on new meaning in our lives. It didn't take long to figure out we needed help—big-time help.

I approached a friend who knew people in the publishing industry and asked if he could help us find a publisher. Six months later we had a contract with Focus on the Family Publishing. They helped us rewrite and expand our book to be re-released in spring of 1989. *A Mother's Manual for Summer Survival* became an instant bestseller. (As of this writing, it has now sold more than 375,000 copies.) The next year we wrote the obvious sequel—*A Mother's Manual for Schoolday Survival*. It too made the bestseller list quickly.

A good friend in Fort Worth, Judie Byrd, and I began planning a project entitled *A Mother's Manual for Holiday Survival* using hundreds of ideas from her food and entertaining school which she teaches from her home. This book also evolved into a how-to video series.

What started with a step of faith to pursue a desire I felt God had placed within my heart, has now evolved into a corporation committed to providing creative resources to strengthen busy families. Books, videos, magazine articles, marketing meetings, seminars, television, and radio—every day brings something different, and I love it.

One thing that makes my job easier is my incredibly flexible and supportive husband. As president of a ministry that mentors business people, Bill spends a great deal of his time teaching men and women the value of their daily work in God's eyes. He also helps them discover where they fit in God's plan. I have picked up a lot of my perspective on work from Bill.

As a budding entrepreneur I have learned that my work is God's gift to me. God has given men and women the privilege of working with him to meet the needs of the world. Not just spiritual needs, but physical and emotional needs are important to him as well. Paul writes "*Whatever you do, work at it with all your heart, as working for the Lord, not for men, since you know that you will receive* an inheritance from the Lord as a reward. It is the Lord Christ you are serving" (Col. 3:23–24, emphasis mine). *Whatever* job I perform—whether changing a diaper, closing a deal, teaching a class, or writing a book—when I meet legitimate needs, I am carrying on God's work. I work for the same reason I go to church—to worship God and serve my fellow man. Whether I am singing a hymn or signing a contract, it is significant to him. My high calling then is to do the will of my Father, whether I am in a boardroom, a bedroom, or a Bible study. "*Whatever* you do, whether in word or deed, do it all in the name of the Lord Jesus, giving thanks to God the Father through him" (Col. 3:17, emphasis mine).

The most valuable lesson I learned from Bill, though, is that the incredible rush of pleasure I feel after turning in a manuscript or speaking to a large group of women is the smile of God in my life. It is not something I need to apologize for. When we find what God created us to do, it pleases him, producing an inner joy in us that comes directly from employing the gifts God has given. I can't tell you what a relief it was to learn that I don't have to feel guilty for hating to clean house, cook, and exchange casserole recipes. God created me for something else. It's all right that I love some things the so-called model Christian woman is not supposed to enjoy.

Like everyone else, I have to do things I don't enjoy sometimes, but I don't have to love them. In Ephesians 2:10, Paul tells us, "For we are God's workmanship, created in Christ Jesus to do good works, which God prepared in advance for us to do." I didn't acquire these gifts myself. Yes it's true I would rather write a marketing plan than bake a cake. This is the way God put me together. He had certain accomplishments in mind when he created me, and he gave me the equipment I needed to do the work.

According to Romans 12:3–7, our gifts are our calling. It is God's will for us to function in the areas of our God-given strengths. Since God's will is the source of joy (Nehemiah 8:10), following your joy is a great way to discover your gifts and God's will for your life. In Ecclesiastes 5:18–19 Solomon commented: "Then I realized that it is good and proper for a man to eat and drink, and to find satisfaction in his toilsome labor under the sun during the few days of life God has given him—for this is his lot. Moreover, when God gives any man wealth and possessions, and enables him to enjoy them, to accept his lot and be happy in his work—this is a gift of God."

Something else I've had to learn is to not be overly impressed with myself. I confess that it's a pretty big rush to do a segment on "Good Morning America" or "The Home Show." Yes, it's fun to be picked up in a limousine and pampered by the network hair stylist and makeup artist. And to see my books on bestseller lists and my articles printed in major magazines is quite a thrill. I'm afraid I've had to do battle with the big-head syndrome more than a few times. But when I remember why I am here, it brings me back to reality. Yes, I am a gifted person, but so is everyone else. And where, pray tell, did I get these gifts I use to do my work? Sure, I have worked very hard. But who gave me the energy to work? And who controlled all the other variables that contributed to my success? The main reason for the measure of my success is not what I have done, but what God has done for me and through me. He is the boss of this outfit. I work for him.

Here's the bottom line. I have numerous responsibilities before God . . . some are glamorous, some are mundane. But they are all important. I can't ignore my husband's need for attention because that's less exciting than a big speaking engagement. I can't disregard my teenager's request to type a book report because I'm writing a magazine article that seems more significant. And it's just as important for me to help my first-grader find the perfect "show and tell" as it is to come up with a perfect chapter title in this book. I am able to change roles because I know it is God's will for me to balance my family responsibilities with my work. Although I am thankful for my career, being a good wife and mom is as important as anything else I do. Whatever work God gives me to do, whether at home or in the marketplace, I pray daily he will help me do it well. He will have to, because I can't do it alone. "Unless the Lord builds the house, its builders labor in vain. Unless the Lord watches over the city, the watchmen stand guard in vain" (Ps. 127:1).

Because my business has grown so rapidly, I've been on a sharp learning curve for the past four years. I've read countless books about business and marketing, studied the Bible to learn what God says about business, relationships, and finances, and sought out mentors to learn from and model my life after. One of the most influential people in my business is my father. I sat down one day and wrote the Big Eight principles of good business I learned from him and other mentors.

The Big Eight

1. A good name is better than silver and gold.
2. Always deliver more than you promise.
3. Honesty is always the best policy.
4. Get-rich-quick schemes don't work. There's no substitute for hard work, discipline, and prayer.
5. The early bird not only catches the worm, but also puts in a half-day's work before the rest of the world gets up.

6. Never stop learning. Readers are leaders, and leaders are readers.

7. Appreciate the people who work for you and with you.

8. Strive for excellence, but not perfection.

I've found the Book of Proverbs to be an excellent operating manual for any profession. Although there are countless verses in Proverbs that have affected my philosophy about work, discipline, ethics, money, and business relationships, there is one verse I designated to be the motto for my career: "The horse is made ready for the day of battle, but victory rests with the Lord" (Prov. 21:31). To me, this means I do everything I can to prepare and do my work in an excellent manner—whatever it is. Then I pray and allow God to bring about victory and blessing in the areas and projects he chooses. It's reassuring to know he is the blessed controller of all things; although on days like today I wonder if I'm on his list of children who need a little more control than others.

All this ran through my head on that trip from Denver to Dallas. As the pilot made his final approach I awoke from my half-dream state and felt my internal homing device at work. I was ready to be safe and sound in my own bed. The adventure wasn't over, however. Since the plane arrived in Dallas more than two hours behind schedule, I ran as fast as I could to my connecting gate. (All travelers know that the shorter the layover, the longer the distance will be to your connecting flight gate. I think the airlines plan it that way.) Panting and perspiring profusely, I finally made it. "Sorry I'm late." I tried to smile.

"I am too," the gate agent responded. "Your plane just left." I laid my head on the ticket counter and tried not to cry.

"So when's the next flight?" I calmly inquired.

"Tomorrow morning at 8:30," he answered without emotion.

Well, I guess every job has its downside, I thought. I'll just have to make the best of it.

I rented a car at the airport and began the two-hour drive home. When I walked into the house at 1:45 A.M., Bill met me at the door. After a big hug I said, "Honey, I think I want to go back to college and major in home economics. Maybe I could learn to be a good homemaker or even learn another trade—one that doesn't require travel."

Bill smiled when he responded, "Don't give me that line. You'll be at your computer tomorrow morning probably writing about what happened to you today."

Daily Disciplines

"Let every man or woman work out the thing that is in him. Whoever uses the means that he has, great or small, and does the work that is given him to do, stands by the side of Jesus and is a fellow worker with Him"— George MacDonald.

When we're feeling desperate about our work— whether it's doing the tenth load of dirty clothes, closing an important deal, or sorting through a knotty conflict— it is crucial to focus on the relationship our work has to God's work. If we are meeting legitimate needs, our work is God's work. We are partners with him in the ongoing care and development of his universe. He asks us to do our best, but never alone. We are standing beside Jesus joining him in the joy of participating in work he created us to do.

What does this mean? He is present when you need help. He is as adept in your laundry room or boardroom as at church. Because it is his work, he is a remarkable source of wisdom for any difficult problem you might face. All you have to do is ask. Because you are his design, he is your best source of guidance as you choose your tasks.

Whatever your work now or whatever you want to create for yourself in the future, you must follow the design God placed within you. Even though there will always be tasks in our lives that are less than exciting, God's will is for us to find the work that brings to us the pleasure of doing what he created us to do. Because it is so easy to fall into the trap of doing what we "must" and "should" do rather than our "heart's desire," many of the expressions here focus on surfacing the things that God has put within us. Pick and choose the ones which apply to your life now. Some of them can be done on a daily basis. Some at frequent intervals. Remember, you can't do them all. (That wouldn't be using your talents wisely; you probably wouldn't get anything else done.)

> ❦ "The real indication that you are where God wants you to be is not only the inner joy that he is using your strengths, but the humility that comes from knowing how much he is doing in spite of your weaknesses"—Bill Peel. What have you seen lately that God has done in spite of your weaknesses? Thank him.

> ❦ Try to do your business by this philosophy: "I come to the office each morning and stay for long hours doing what has to be done to the best of my ability. And when you've done the best you can, you can't do any better. So when I go to sleep I turn everything over to the Lord and forget it"—Harry S Truman.

- ❦ "May he give you the desire of your heart and make all your plans succeed" (Ps. 20:4). Write out your plans in your prayer journal and pray about them regularly.

- ❦ Don't be afraid of hard work. "Opportunity is missed by most people because it is dressed in overalls and looks like work"—Thomas A. Edison.

- ❦ Be a person of your word to the best of your ability.

- ❦ Read *Leadership Is an Art,* by Max Dupree.

- ❦ "Nothing great was ever achieved without enthusiasm"—Ralph Waldo Emerson. Discover the enthusiasm within you. What do you get excited about?

- ❦ Send thank-you notes to those people who help you in your work.

- ❦ Make your desk or work environment as pleasant as possible. I keep favorite pictures of family and friends on my desk. I also have my favorite books close at hand, as well as colorful office supplies.

- ❦ Think about this:

  The heights by great men reached and kept
      Were not attained by sudden flight,
  But they, while their companions slept,
      Were toiling upward in the night.
          Henry Wadsworth Longfellow

- ❦ If you do sloppy or mediocre work, this forms an image about you within the recipient. Always make sure you send out your best effort. Take a little extra time to do it right.

❧ Read the book *Love and Profit,* by James A. Autry. He says that almost all business is lost because of relationship problems. Do your part to maintain healthy business relationships.

❧ Make friends with people who stimulate and motivate you. Learn from them.

❧ "He is well paid who is well satisfied"—William Shakespeare. What is well paid for you? It might be a kindergartner saying, "Thanks, Mommy, for a great birthday party," or it might be the first paycheck at your new job.

❧ No matter what your career, do it with a sense of high calling. You influence the atmosphere and character of everyone around you, whether at an office, a plant, or at home.

❧ Read *You Don't Have to Go Home from Work Exhausted,* by Dr. Ann McGee-Cooper.

❧ Pursue creative outlets when you feel bogged down in your work. I play a sonata or read a chapter in a stimulating book when I need to be refreshed.

❧ Whatever your work, do it for God. "Teach me, my God and King, in all things thee to see, and what I do in any thing, to do it as for thee"—George Herbert.

❧ When you're feeling down, take some time to write down the people you influence. Or get out your file of notes and cards from people you've helped or influenced. If you don't have a file, start one.

❧ Is there something you can do today that will prepare you for something you want to do in the future?

❦ Be dependable . . . to yourself as well as others. Know that others can depend on you to do what you promise to or need to. And depend on yourself to do something that pleases you each and every day.

❦ "Every man's work, whether it be literature or music or pictures or architecture or anything else, is always a portrait of himself"—Samuel Butler. What does your work say about you?

❦ Look people in the eye when you're doing business with them.

❦ Try to remember first names and something about each person you meet. Keep a file of important information about business associates.

❦ Give yourself the freedom to daydream. I learned from a lecture by Dr. Ann McGee-Cooper that astronauts in training at NASA are required to learn to daydream—an important skill for anyone who might need to think creatively in a critical situation. They start off by daydreaming twenty minutes and build up to two hours.

❦ Make sure your values have more weight in making a business decision than your impulses or desires.

❦ Dave Thomas, CEO of Wendy's, attributes his success to honesty, integrity, hard work, and a strong desire for success. What words would you use to describe your career?

❦ There are twenty-eight Proverbs that talk about the glory or benefits of hard work. Read them.

❦ "A good reputation is more valuable than money"—Publilius Syrus. Never forget this.

❦ Ask yourself: What am I passionate about? and What is stopping me from pursuing my passion?

❦ "Much has been given us, and much will rightfully be expected from us. We have duties to others and duties to ourselves; and we can shirk neither"—Theodore Roosevelt. What does this mean in your life?

❦ "Whatever it is, however impossible it seems, whatever the obstacles that stand between you and it, if it is noble, if it is consistent with God's kingdom, you hunger after it. You must stretch yourself to reach it"—Charles Cohn. Is there something you want to reach? Do it.

❦ Be innovative. If you're not ahead of the crowd, you'll soon be behind it.

❦ Remember all of life is sacred. Whether you're washing dishes, changing a diaper, or writing a sales contract, "Whatever you do, whether in word or deed, do it all in the name of the Lord Jesus, giving thanks to God the Father through him" (Col. 3:17).

❦ Using the gifts God gave you brings joy, energy, and enthusiasm. When you function in the area of your God-given abilities, you engage God's creative power. There is no deeper satisfaction than doing what he desires. Each of us has a responsibility to discern our God-given gifts. Read *The Truth About You*, by Arthur Miller and Ralph Mattson to help you discover your gifts.

- ❧ "Great deeds are usually wrought at great risks"—Herodotus. Is there something you have always wanted to do, but you're afraid to take the risk? What's stopping you?

- ❧ Do common things uncommonly well. List ten common things you do uncommonly well.

- ❧ "Good leadership is getting people to do what they don't want to do in order to achieve what they want to achieve"—Tom Landry. This principle applies at the office or at home. How can you apply it to your life on a daily basis?

- ❧ Think about this: "Do not wear yourself out to get rich; have the wisdom to show restraint. Cast but a glance at riches, and they are gone, for they will surely sprout wings and fly off to the sky like an eagle" (Prov. 23:4–5).

Self-Disciplines

- ❧ Pick a favorite spot where you can spend some quiet time alone. Meditate on Psalm 37:4, "Delight yourself in the Lord and he will give you the desires of your heart." Write down the desires of your heart.

Part 2

Confessions of a
Desperate Wife

5

Not Tonight, I Have a Headache

*B*ill and I are in the people-consulting business. He is president of Foundations for Living, a cross-denominational ministry to business people in East Texas. He also helps people understand how to focus their energy on what God created them to do. I am president of Creative People, Inc., a company committed to providing creative resources to strengthen busy families. Whether we like it or not, since we get involved with counseling people about their work lives and that relates to their private lives, sometimes marriage counseling comes with the territory. Bill, by virtue of his personality, listens patiently and cares sincerely about the people he works with. Tenderly, but firmly, he cuts through surface issues and gets to the root problems.

I, on the other hand, listen to one side of the story four to five minutes tops, then look appalled and am tempted to blurt out, "You jerk . . . I can't believe you did that!"—not what someone with problems needs to hear. When asked to sit in on a counseling conversation, I strive to keep my smart-alecky comments to myself. Instead, I try to offer creative solutions to the problem and help folks laugh at themselves. Over the years, I've heard some great stories. Bedroom stories are among the best.

We've laughed with many a couple whose first night as husband and wife was not exactly a scene from "Fantasy Island." For example, take Diane and Ken (not their real names). Their wedding day started with a major conflict between Diane and her mother. Ken could not understand why she cried during the entire two-hour drive from the church to the hotel. She dried her eyes when they checked in. Ready to move on with the anticipated events of the evening, Ken carried her over the threshold into a room filled with modern walnut furniture.

Diane burst into tears again. It seems she had always dreamed of spending her wedding night on a white French Provincial bed. Ken, who also had dreams of what his wedding night would be like, spent the next two hours going from room to room with the hotel manager, hellbent on finding white French Provincial furniture. Exhausted, they finally moved their belongings into their new room at 3:00 A.M. I'm not sure what transpired after that, but they do have two children now.

It was all I could do to keep a straight face when our friend Paul recounted how he sat on the king-size bed and nervously waited for Barbara to emerge from the hotel bathroom on their first night. When she made her appearance, he did a double take and questioned whether he had whisked the right woman away in the getaway car. He didn't recognize her without makeup, two wiglets, and false eyelashes. He never imagined she would "take it all off" . . . literally.

And many newlyweds, wanting to carefully plan the timing of their first child, are a little nervous about practicing birth control. Mike and Patty can look back now and smile about their first year of marriage. But at first Patty was terrified of getting pregnant. Mike tried to be patient, but thought it was a little bit of an overkill that she insisted on using three different kinds of birth control—simultaneously—every time they made love.

But of all the great bedroom accounts I've ever listened in on, I must admit that the following was an approach I'd never heard . . . and probably one I won't recommend to anyone in the future. Stan and Rhonda were on the fast track—living in two separate worlds. After ten years of marriage, they hardly ever saw each other. He seldom gave her any attention, but wanted sex. She seldom gave him any sex, but wanted attention.

During our second meeting, Rhonda looked across the table at Stan and screamed, "You don't care about anything but sex. If you really cared about *me,* you'd show me your love by giving me some of your precious time . . . and a few gifts every once in a while as well!"

Well, Stan was a creative kind of guy, and a smart aleck as well. He fumed, "Okay, she wants attention? She's got it. She wants a gift? She's got that too." He left work early one afternoon and went home. He knew Rhonda would arrive around two o'clock, and the children would still be at school.

When she came home, she walked into the bedroom and found Stan totally naked, lying on the bed with a bright red gift bow strategically tied around one of his appendages.

Needless to say, Rhonda did not appreciate Stan's "thoughtful" gift, and next week's session was volatile.

It's fun to sit back and laugh at these stories now. But there was a time in my life when I couldn't crack a smile about the sexual aspect of our marriage. Not unlike many married women, I went through a period when I did not enjoy our sexual relationship at all. For me, sexual intercourse ranked right up there with cleaning the oven.

There are several emotional factors that affect my womanly feelings about my sexual relationship with Bill.

They include my sense of security and acceptance, my surroundings, the everyday stress of motherhood, the highs and lows of work, my health, difficult circumstances, the way Bill treats me and shows me his love, to mention a few. Unfortunately, most of these are things I can't control. It would be wonderful if Bill were Prince Charming and we lived in a beautiful castle. Life would be terrific if he never spoke unkind words, if we always had more than enough money, and if the children never got sick in the middle of the night. Unfortunately life's not like that. I tried for years to manipulate Bill into becoming what I wanted him to be. And I attempted to escape negative situations at all costs. I finally realized that I had no power over the uncontrollable circumstances I found myself in. However, I had the choice of whether or not I saw myself as a victim.

When I admitted, for the first time in my marriage, that Bill would never be Prince Charming, it finally dawned on me that what goes on inside me emotionally is much more important to my sex life than what goes on around me. I had to deal with some childhood experiences that colored my perspective. My introduction to sex was through *Playboy* magazines placed carelessly on a neighbor's coffee table for guests to enjoy. Even as an eight-year-old those images left an indelible impression on me and formed my opinion that women were only objects men used for their own pleasure.

A frightening experience with a boy from school during junior high confirmed this and caused further scarring that affected my most fundamental thoughts about sex. Forced into a dark bathroom against my will, I endured a less than pleasant experience. He scared me and gave me a horrible introduction to something beautiful. I was disgusted. This experience stayed with me for years. It flashed before me at the oddest times.

Because of this and my inability to talk with anyone about it, I could not reconcile these impressions and memories with my faith or my role as a wife. Often the thought of sex brought a flood of confusing emotions. My strong desires to please my husband and enjoy the pleasures of sexual intimacy were constantly bombarded and threatened by my feelings of anger and guilt.

As I wrestled with overcoming my feelings I blamed God in anger. "How could you let something so disgusting happen to me? Why did my introduction to sex have to be so negative?"

In addition to inner conflicts, physical exhaustion also played a major part in my lack of sexual interest. The demands of motherhood and teaching school were almost more than I could handle. After our second child was born, I felt brain dead and sensually numb by the time nine o'clock rolled around. Once in bed, the only thing I wanted to do was sleep.

Another factor made the situation even worse. I had a bad case of misplaced priorities. My definition of a devoted Christian woman included attending every Bible study offered, being present at the church every time the doors were open, and volunteering my time to less fortunate people in the community. My impressive agenda almost destroyed my marriage. Any time and energy I had left over after mothering and chauffeuring the children, I gave to everyone else except Bill. One week I looked at my calendar and counted three Bible studies, a Bible memory group, a ladies' fellowship group at the church, and two community project meetings. I was out saving the world while my husband's needs remained unmet. I appeared to be the model Christian woman, yet stress continued to build in our marriage. Living a life of deception, I came close to the breaking point. I finally forced myself to stop long enough to take stock of my life.

I had to face the reality that these activities served as an escape from the pain involved in developing the full relationship God desired for Bill and me.

As I've mentioned before, I am a fighter and don't like to give up or admit defeat in anything. For both of us, I wanted our sexual relationship to be all it could be. I wanted to be a wonderful wife to Bill, and I knew I too was missing out on the joy of physical intimacy. So I began to study, hoping to find some answers. In the Book of Genesis, I read that sex was God's idea, not a product of male lust. God intended for Adam and Eve to enjoy the beauty and pleasure of sex. The warmth and openness expressed in Genesis 2:25 spoke not only to my deep inner longings, but to the sexual part of me as well. "The man and his wife were naked, and they felt no shame."

In Psalm 45, the writer describes a royal wedding where the king and queen are exhorted to look upon and desire each other's beauty. The Song of Solomon is downright sensual! And the description of marital love in Proverbs 5:18–19 is graphic to say the least: "May your fountain be blessed, and may you rejoice in the wife of your youth. A loving doe, a graceful deer—may her breasts satisfy you always, may you ever be captivated by her love." It was also encouraging to read that God had commanded a new husband to make the sexual pleasure of his new wife a chief priority. "If a man has recently married, he must not be sent to war or have any other duty laid on him. For one year he is to be free to stay at home and bring happiness to the wife he has married" (Deut. 24:5).

The more passages I read, the clearer it became that as husband and wife, we not only have a responsibility to please each other, but the privilege of being pleased in return. The pleasure of sex is a beautiful gift from God to be enjoyed by husband and wife. My earlier negative perceptions stemmed from Satan's perversions. As I realized this, I wanted desperately to experience God's gift as he intended it.

I declared war and entered the battle proactively. This was not a fight for self-change using the power of positive thinking, but a battle of faith. Faith in God to heal my hurts from the past, renew my mind with his perspective, and restore affection for my husband. To my surprise I found God had already declared war on these strongholds of perverted thought and was waiting for my permission to retake captive areas of my mind.

You're probably wanting me to tell you I experienced a miraculous overnight recovery and awoke the next morning with irrepressible libido. It didn't happen that way. Like most worthwhile things, it took time, prayer, and commitment. God dealt with me patiently and lovingly. He taught me some important lessons about his healing power and the discipline of my thoughts and time.

First, I prayed for God to erase the negative pictures etched on my mind. I poured out my feelings and requests to God honestly, but wondered how he could turn these memories into something positive. During an early morning quiet time, the Lord directed me to a verse of scripture I had probably read a hundred times before and even memorized. But this time I read the next verse too. It was as though the light came on for the first time. Stunned, I read, "And we know that in all things God works for the good of those who love him, who have been called according to his purpose. For those God foreknew he also predestined to be conformed to the likeness of his Son" (Rom. 8:28–29).

Until this point, I *read* verse 28 as it was printed, but actually *believed* the verse meant God probably would work *some* of the circumstances in my life for good and I would just have to make the most of the rest. When I entertained the possibility that God would actually work *all* things in my life—the good, the bad, and the ugly—to make me more like Jesus Christ, I saw my painful past from a completely new angle. Over time I was able to let go of angry feelings about what had happened to me as I believed God could somehow use this incident for good to transform me into the image of Christ. My new understanding released me from the burden of years of guilt and anger.

I also began the process that the Apostle Paul calls "the renewing of your mind" (Romans 12:2). As I read and studied the Bible and sound theological books about God's perspective on sex, my thoughts and feelings were slowly but radically changed. I discovered that my sexual intimacy actually begins in my brain!

I found I not only had to put truth into my mind aggressively, but I had to guard against putting any more trash into it as well. Although tempted to take a shortcut to pleasure, I did not allow myself to be pulled into the soap-opera, R-rated-movie, or sexy-novel method of thinking romantic thoughts. I am convinced that grazing mentally on illicit relationships can result in bad spiritual indigestion. The consequences of adulterous relationships are never mentioned in these books and programs, and women who allow themselves to fantasize about men who do not really exist harm their marriages. There is no way any husband can compete with a perfect character created by a Hollywood producer. As she focuses on a fantasy, it only causes the wife to see the flaws in her mate rather than his strengths—producing anything but affection.

As I continued my study of the Scriptures, I began to gain an understanding of what true affection really is. In Phillipians 1:8, Paul wrote that he longed for his friends in Phillipi with the affection of Christ Jesus. I turned this verse into a personal prayer for my marriage by praying that Christ Jesus would be the source of my affections. I wanted to long for my husband in the way God created a woman to desire a man. He answered this prayer graciously.

Not only did my thought patterns about sex need to be overhauled, but I needed a fresh understanding about what it means to be a woman. In a culture well on its way to closing the gender gap between men and women, there is a danger in devaluing the differences between men and women. I wanted to emphasize the differences by celebrating my femininity. I thought purposefully in new ways about myself and the way God created me. In the first chapter of Genesis, mankind is clearly the pinnacle of God's creation. The second chapter retells the individual creation of man and then woman, using different words for the creation of man and woman. In verse 7, he "formed" man. In verse 22, he "fashioned" woman. This describes the great care a master craftsman uses to create a fine piece of art.

God created both men and women—to be themselves—different from each other in order to bring pleasure to each other, and to give each other, in a variety of almost countless ways, what the other lacks. We have so long undervalued women and femininity that this is almost lost.

When I realized that God created women magnificently, not as an afterthought, I began to rejoice in the beauty and mystique of my femininity with a new awareness of my sexuality and the unique beauty God gave woman. The more feminine I felt, the more romantic I wanted to be with my husband. It was a wonderful feeling!

Although I was making progress in forming a new perspective, I was often too exhausted to act upon my newfound emotions. Although I was not working at a career at this time, I filled my days with many *good* activities. The grueling schedule I kept sapped every ounce of my energy. An older woman in our church wisely discerned my struggle, took me aside, and gave me some loving advice. She said, "Kathy, you have a good heart, but your priorities are out of line. Being a Christian wife means saying no sometimes to many worthwhile projects, Bible studies, and efforts to evangelize the world, so you can concentrate on the needs in your marriage. You can be a testimony of God's power and goodness to your quick-divorce generation by just staying together—and not just enduring your relationship, but enjoying it." She continued, "God created marriage to be a blessing not a curse! You need to take care of that sweet husband God gave you. The witness of a good marriage will have a much greater impact on the world than a head full of Bible knowledge and a schedule full of good deeds."

I knew she was right. Painful though it was, I got out my pen, marked out meetings on my calendar, and resigned from two organizations. I also tried to be sensitive to Bill's needs. If I thought he might be looking forward to spending a romantic evening together, I rested a little during the day to be fresh for him at night. Even when the children outgrew their nap times, I required them to play or read quietly in their rooms so that I could recharge my personal batteries. I used this time to contemplate romantic thoughts. I envisioned Bill and myself experiencing a beautiful time of enjoying each other physically. This prepared me for our evening together after the kids went to bed.

I shared the story of my sexual awakening with a woman who was sexually cold and filled with resentment toward her husband. She refused to forgive him for hurting her in the past. Angry and upset, she lashed out,

"Who are you anyway—Pollyanna? Get real! You're nothing but a doormat."

The lines in her face revealed pent-up bitterness. Her countenance had hardened. I answered her outburst by saying up front that I couldn't pretend to understand her pain and that I did not have all the answers. I also wanted her to know I am not a doormat, nor do I have a Pollyanna lifestyle. I struggle with more problems than I can possibly handle on a daily basis. And Bill consistently disappoints my picture of the ideal husband (which he readily admits). But he's not the issue, I am.

In my struggles and searching I've found that God always gives me the ability to do his will. When I step out in faith wanting to obey the principles in his Word, he blesses my feeble attempts at obedience, though this often goes against my feelings and the counsel of the world. When I set out to reawaken my own sensuality, I did it out of a profound longing to connect deeply with my husband. I didn't do it to try to please myself or so I could please Bill so he'd do something for me.

Modern society often tells me to look out for my own happiness, seek personal fulfillment first, and satisfy my own desires at all costs. My experience is that this is the quickest way to end up unfulfilled and miserable. Jesus said, "For whoever wants to save his life will lose it, but whoever loses his life for me and for the gospel will save it" (Mark 8:35). When I put myself first, I am tempted to try to change Bill into what I think he should be—usually like me in some way. This is really a form of self-idolatry—setting myself up as the standard to which he should conform. It's a plan that always backfires, and we lose ground in our relationship. The Bible tells me not to win him over with talk, but by my Christlike behavior (1 Pet. 3:1–2). God and Bill are responsible for Bill's behavior; I'm not. (Amazingly, God sometimes uses a wife's godliness to effect change in her husband, but this should never be the motive.) Likewise, God and I are responsible for my behavior.

Although I'm thankful for the progress I've made, striving to be a good wife continues to be a daily struggle. My self-centered and independent spirit raises its ugly head at regular intervals. It seems as though I get one area somewhat under control, then I discover there is another part of our relationship where I am failing miserably.

I look at my role in our marriage like riding a bicycle. I must keep pedaling and moving forward. Otherwise I'll lose my balance and fall off. Some roads I travel are like a delightful slope I can coast down, enjoying the fresh breeze against my face. Other roads have steep hills that take every ounce of my strength to climb. There are days when I wonder if I'll make it to the other side. Commitment to get over the hill, no matter how intense the pain, is many times the only way I make it. I crash regularly and injure myself as well as Bill in the process. But the vow I made twenty-one years ago reminds me to get up, brush myself off, and keep pedaling.

God uses several ways to help me in my efforts to be a good wife. One is the encouragement of two close friends. On a girls' getaway to Colorado a few years ago, we shared some of our desires and defeats as wives.

After morning coffee, a devotional, and prayer, as is our custom, we commented on how we were all in the "mid-life crisis" stage of life. We talked about the trend of middle-aged men trying to find their "trophy wife." This woman is often quite a few years younger than her husband, beautiful, and accomplished in her own right. Many men feel their trophy wife will enhance their career status and affirm their masculinity. She is their fantasy mistress and ultimate movie star. She's the red convertible they always lusted after and the cheerleader who wouldn't give them a second glance.

Behind this perverted view of their manhood, I believe, is a God-given desire by men to be respected and honored. A man also wants a woman he can be proud of and who is proud to be with him. God has placed this desire in the heart of every man. Of course it can be and often is twisted. Men are at their lowest point when they demand or try to take this respect by a show of force. Nonetheless, it is part of their design, and provides a real key to ministering to them in a way that touches their deepest being.

While in Colorado, we formed the Trophy Wives Club. We encourage one another to be good wives. We share tactics that have worked in our own marriage. And we pass on information about good lingerie sales. (Our husbands love this part of our club!) Drawing from our own experiences, we brainstormed about specific ways we could be trophy wives in a positive sense, so our husbands wouldn't feel the need to look for someone else.

Although many ideas applied to all three of us, we realized we each need to be students of our own husbands and strive to know their deepest needs. Each man is unique and what's important to one might be low on the priority list of another. We made a pact that we would each go home and try to be trophy wives to our husbands. Since that day we have held each other accountable for the decision. None of us has a perfect marriage, and we all struggle regularly. But we're committed to working hard on making it the best it can be. Many of the expressions of spiritual discipline which follow come from this ongoing fellowship of wives.

Daily Disciplines

"The greatest discovery of my generation is that people can alter their lives by altering their attitudes"— William James.

What was true for William James's generation is still true today. We can alter our lives by altering our attitudes. Wanting to change the way we relate to our husbands, particularly sexually, often requires that we change the way we think about them and the way we think about ourselves. Altering my attitude can mean taking care of myself and my body so I feel more sensual, more ready to connect intimately. It can mean altering the way I interact with my husband so he sees that I'm different.

All of the suggestions here are made with an eye toward helping you alter your attitude and your life. They're all ways to invite your husband, yourself, and God into your physical life—even if they don't seem like they have anything to do with your husband or God.

Pick and choose from this list, doing what appeals to you. There's no right or wrong way to choose. You don't get more points for trying to do most or all of the things on this list, especially every day. If you were to try that, what you'd probably get would be exhaustion. Many of them are designed to do occasionally. You can plan ahead for them, and savor the anticipation.

- ❧ Talk openly about how you like to be touched. Learn what your husband enjoys. By pleasing him, you will receive pleasure too.

- ❧ If you have an ugly or frightening experience etched on your memory, ask God to help forgive the person who hurt you and show you how this negative experience can be used in a positive way in your life.

- ❧ Find a cologne for you and an aftershave lotion for him that you both like. Wear it every day.

❦ Together read some of the Bible verses mentioned in this chapter. Talk about what they mean to you.

❦ Keep up with current events and be a good conversationalist.

❦ Make an affirmation list about yourself. Include the reasons your husband was attracted to you in the first place. Reclaim some of those in your daily life.

❦ Buy sexy underwear and wear it regularly.

❦ Plan a surprise overnight outing at a hotel. Take a tape player and romantic music. Dance in your room. Or if your husband doesn't like surprises, savor the planning of such a wonderful weekend together. "Romantic love is good medicine for fears and anxieties and a low self-image. Psychologists point out that real romantic love has an organizing and constructive effect on our personalities. It brings out the best in us, giving us the will to improve ourselves and to reach for a greater maturity and responsibility. This love enables us to begin to function at our highest level"— Dr. Ed Wheat, *Love Life for Every Married Couple.*

❦ Collect fragrant soaps and bubble baths. Treat yourself regularly to a relaxing bath. You'll feel feminine and refreshed.

❦ Surprise your husband with a new pair of boxer shorts. Give him a red and white pair on Valentine's Day.

❦ Meditate daily on how God created men and women. Write your own prayer of affirmation.

❦ Farm out the kids one night and fix a candle-light dinner. Nicely explain to your husband that the kids are very demanding and you would really appreciate his help with them when he gets home from work. This way you can save some of your energy for him.

❦ Treat yourself to a manicure, or a new hairdo, or a massage. You'll feel more beautiful.

❦ Collect pretty bed clothes and robes.

❦ ". . . whatever is true, whatever is noble, whatever is right, whatever is pure, whatever is lovely, whatever is admirable—if anything is excellent or praiseworthy—think about such things" (Phil. 4:8). Ask God to help you focus your thoughts on good things, rather than on bad experiences from the past. Fill your mind regularly with Scripture and good literature.

❦ Show interest in your husband's work. Think of ways you can be a trophy wife to him in his business. This could be by dressing spectacularly for an office party. By talking intelligently with his colleagues at a dinner. Or by giving your husband something great to talk about at the office.

❦ Use fragrant bath powders every morning and night. Moisturize your skin with lotion at least once a day. The older we get, the more moisture our skin requires to stay soft.

❦ Give yourself regular pedicures. Keep dead skin and callouses rubbed off. Polish your toenails a pretty color.

❦ Exercise regularly. A woman I know shared that when she began regularly attending an aerobics dance class, her husband noticed a sharp rise in her energy level and libido. He gladly pays for her to continue the class.

❦ Try to look your best every day. One husband confessed to Bill he resented his wife's sloppy warmup suits and unkempt look. His work required him to do business with attractive, well-dressed professional women. His wife's appearance in the morning and when he returned home in the afternoon was not very enticing.

❦ Pray together regularly. This promotes intimacy as a couple.

❦ Strive to make wise decisions about what forms of entertainment you allow yourself to watch or participate in. Do not purposely put yourself in situations that bring to mind negative situations from your past. If this happens, ask God to help you not fall into old thought patterns.

❦ Call your spouse on the phone in the middle of the day. Talk to him in a sexy voice. Ask him if he'd like to make a date for later in the evening.

❦ Wrap up in your favorite quilt and go to bed for a twenty-minute rest. Think about a favorite intimate memory.

❦ Make your bedroom as romantic as possible.

❦ Plan a romantic rendezvous and be creative. Don't get in the rut of making love in the same place in the same way at the same time. Do something out of the ordinary—pull your mate into a closet for a passionate kiss, watch a sunset together from a boat in the remote part of a lake, go parking. Remember, you're married and it's legal!

❦ If your husband travels, spray cotton balls with your cologne and put them in a zip-lock bag. Hide the bag in his suitcase with a love note. He can remember your scent although you're miles away.

❦ Give each other space. Getting away from each other for a few days can be very healthy. It's a wonderful feeling to miss someone. When you're away from your normal routine you can gain a fresh perspective.

❦ Ask your husband to come home for a special lunch. A friend of mine told me that when her children are in school, she regularly invites her husband home for a midday romantic interlude and meets him at the door in sensual clothes. She wants to make sure he thinks lunch with her is more exciting than lunch with the girls at the office.

❦ Don't take each other for granted. Be discreet with your personal hygiene and bathroom habits. Too much familiarity can ruin an atmosphere of romance.

❦ Plan a "couple's holiday" at home if the kids are spending the night out and you can't get away to a hotel. Turn off the phone, rent an old romantic movie, stock your refrigerator with special snacks, order "room service" and serve each other. Buy a new nightie, have trays ready for breakfast in bed the next morning, buy new magazines and newspapers to read, then relax and have fun.

❦ When your husband comments on an item of women's clothing or lingerie in an advertisement, take note and buy one for yourself.

❦ Live as lovers. Think about what a man would desire in a mistress. Be that person to your husband so he won't ever feel the need for one.

❦ Write your husband a love letter and send it through the mail.

❦ Take a picture of yourselves on a romantic getaway. Frame it and put it on your desk to capture the memory.

❦ Place potpourri and scented candles in your bedroom to give it an enticing fragrance.

❦ If possible, don't fight in the bedroom. Work through your conflicts in another room and save your bedroom for pleasant moments. (Don't fight in front of the children though, unless you make it a point to let them see you make up.)

❦ Put a lock on your bedroom door and use it.

❦ After the kids go to bed, spend a quiet evening together listening to good music and reading your favorite book. Turn off the television.

❦ Go on a picnic together at a pretty park. Pack a quilt, interesting food, and pretty dishes to create a romantic atmosphere.

❦ Start a fantasy vacation file and bank account. Save up for a special trip for just the two of you.

❦ Let the element of surprise add excitement to your relationship. Fight monotony.

❦ Return to a favorite spot you enjoyed while dating. Reminisce about your courtship.

❦ If you feel your eyes wandering toward other men, remember the grass may look greener on the other side, but it still needs mowing.

❦ Enhance the romantic atmosphere in your bedroom by putting a string of little white lights in a ficus tree.

❦ Be careful what you daydream and think about. We talk to ourselves at a rate of thirteen hundred words per minute. As far as my subconscious is concerned, what I say to myself is true because it can't discern between real and imagined.

❦ If you feel your affection waning, ask God to rekindle the fire in your marriage.

❦ "The husband should fulfill his marital duty to his wife, and likewise the wife to her husband. The wife's body does not belong to her alone but also to her husband. In the same way, the husband's body does not belong to him alone but also to his wife. Do not deprive each other except by mutual consent and for a time, so that you may devote yourselves to prayer" (1 Cor. 7:3–5). Sexual intimacy is God's idea and a beautiful gift to every married couple. Take time to cultivate this part of your relationship. When your love life is healthy, this can help you bear other turbulent parts of your relationship.

Self-Disciplines

❧ Turn Philippians 1:8 into a personal prayer for you and your husband. Ask God to give you the affection of Jesus Christ for each other. Write down specific ideas you've had while reading this chapter that might rekindle romance in your marriage. Do something today.

6

How to Live in Continual Marital Bliss, Plus More Great Fiction

*T*ruth be known, most husbands and wives have at least one touchy topic that causes even those who would never think of divorce to at least consider homicide. Sex and in-laws usually rank in the top five. Money is also popular. Bill and I fight over vacations.

I'm not referring to family vacations. We take wonderful trips with our kids and should probably win the Gloria Gaither-Shirley Dobson *Let's Make a Memory* Award for spending so many positive moments with our children.

We fight over *adult* trips. You know—the dream getaway where you envision yourself on the deck of a cruise ship. In your fantasy you look great in a size-four evening dress. And your husband is wearing a tuxedo, holding you romantically. (He also has hair and looks like Tom Selleck.)

After twenty years of arguments and dozens of expensive personality inventory tests, we finally got to the bottom of why we get so stressed out over where we're going to relieve our stress. We have different ideas about what makes a trip fun.

Don't get me wrong. We always enjoy our twice-a-year retreats once we're there. It's just deciding where to go that makes us want to read each other's obituaries.

Bill's idea of a fun getaway is lying on the beach at Cancun with no one around except the two of us. I remind him that I don't look like the girl wearing the bikini on the brochure, and he doesn't have to worry about me using his stomach for a washboard. "We'd look like a couple of beached whales." I explain, "Besides, we could just buy a couple of lawn chairs, sit out in the backyard, take a laxative, and have the same experience for a lot less money."

I, on the other hand, like to be with other people on vacations. I love to be the catalyst that gets four or five fun-loving couples together for an excursion. Bill doesn't mind this kind of a trip, but his fantasy getaway includes only the two of us clad in skimpy bathing suits, eating food we can't pronounce.

Unfortunately for Bill, submission has never been my strong suit. And for this particular time I'm talking about, it was business as usual. I just wouldn't give in easily on this vacation issue. I pride myself in being a rather creative thinker, so I decided to approach him with a plan that included the best of both worlds. I created a very rational, organized, vacation schedule to try to help him see things from my point of view.

"Okay, Honey," I said, trying not to sound manipulative, "let's predict that we'd spend eight hours each night sleeping. And we'd eat three meals a day—that would be four hours we could spend alone in restaurants. And let's add in sex three times each day, allowing three hours total." (Now I had his attention.) "We'd have nine hours left to be with other couples. Wouldn't that be fun?"

He didn't buy it. I gave in and am now sitting in our cabana-for-two at the beach. And you know what? I love it. I don't need other people around to have a good time. Just sitting here with my husband watching the people at the beach is entertainment enough. Out in chest-deep water there are two honeymooners who will be in an embarrassing predicament if a big wave rolls in. Over by the Anyone Can Parasail sign is a mid-life crisis candidate who looks like he just got off of the Love Boat. (His gold chains are okay, but someone needs to tell him the black bikini probably isn't his best look.) But the greatest scene of all is the retired silver-haired couple walking on the beach holding hands—obviously still in love after all the years.

When our once pasty-white bodies have turned a deep shade of crimson, we know it's time for a new activity. As we discuss possible excursions to take during our vacation-for-two, there's one outing we avoid like the plague. We learned the hard way that the words "museum" and "pleasure" are mutually exclusive. I'm not saying how angry we get at each other, but when was the last time you saw a SWAT team called in to settle a domestic dispute? When at a museum, I like to move quickly, taking in as much as possible in a short time. Bill, also known as Mr. Historical Trivia, is a well-versed history student and enjoys diligently studying each exhibit in detail. "Intense frustration" is not quite strong enough to describe our past museum experiences. There are times when our feelings for each other remind us of scenes from the movie *Die Hard*.

Another volatile issue in our relationship is shopping. Although I realize I'm giving up any claim to Christian Wife of the Year, I must be truthful and admit that going shopping with my husband ranks right up there with getting a root canal. This is not a result of arguing over money or different tastes. The problem is a collision of operating styles. When we shop, our end goal is the same, but the way we get there is completely different.

It took us almost nineteen years to figure out why we overdose on antacids after every shopping trip we take together. We have different methods of making decisions. Bill is an information gatherer. He (very wisely I might add) likes to gather every possible bit of data about a product before making a decision. He likes to shop around and enjoys just browsing in stores. When he needs a pair of slacks, he goes to several men's stores and tries on every pair of slacks in his size. Then he thinks about his purchase and asks my advice (the result of returning too many items I didn't like) before finally writing the check. He would rather take additional time coming to one decision and make sure it is a good decision.

I, on the other hand, walk into a store and intuitively know in a minute or two if it's worth my time to be there. I recognize (or think I do) what I like and don't like immediately. I like to take a risk, make a quick decision, and move on to something else. Sometimes, as you might imagine, I suffer the consequences for my fast decisions. The back of my closet tells the tale. He gets mad at me for being impulsive and impatient. I get mad at him for being slow and indecisive.

Different interests also cause us to roll our eyes at each other. Bill is quite intrigued by computers. In other words DOS is his second language. He reads computer magazines, gets excited over new programs, and loves the latest gizmos. Now I like my computer, mind you, and use it daily. But all I want to know is how to turn it on and off. When he walked into the family room one night starry-eyed and passionately exclaimed he was in "font heaven," I thought, Give me oxygen! The man's grip on reality is getting fragile. And on nights when I stay awake until 1:00 A.M. to watch a Tom Peters' presentation on PBS or keep the reading light on in the bedroom half the night while I finish a marketing book, Bill threatens to reformat *me*.

Another cause for battle in our marriage is driving. Bill should have known he was in trouble when we drove two cars back to Texas after our honeymoon and I arrived an hour earlier than he did. (I told him if he had left *two* hours ahead of me instead of one, we would have timed it perfectly.) To me, driving is a challenge. I want to have fun traveling to our destination without wasting any time on the way. In our family large bladders are a virtue. Our kids are glad God made them boys because when we're on a car trip, they've learned to point and shoot fast during my twenty-second pullovers. I'm not saying how fast I drive, but our kids complain that the only way they can play the ABC billboard game is with a time-lapse camera.

Bill, on the other hand, has the conscience of the pope. If the cruise control happens to malfunction causing the car to go two miles over the speed limit, he turns himself in at the nearest highway patrol. Farmers driving hay balers wave as they pass us when Bill's at the wheel. Needless to say, our driving habits cause a great deal of relational strife—especially on long car trips. Bill's blood pressure rises as he calculates how long it will take me to get to the speed of light. And I grit my teeth while trying to think of ways to put lead implants in his shoes. We figured out that on our annual treks to Colorado, by the time we hit the Continental Divide, there's a major division in our family as well.

You would think that after twenty-one years of sleeping in the same bed, sharing the same tube of toothpaste, and raising the same children, we would understand each other. Wrong. We're living proof that opposites may attract, but they might also write the script for *Murder in Texas—Part 2*.

We still frequently catch ourselves trying to live by the golden rule in our marriage: "Do unto others, as you would have them do unto you." In our misunderstood marriage state, that unfortunately reads: "I'll treat *you* like I want *you* to treat *me*, not how you want to be treated." Our fortieth birthday parties are a perfect example.

Bill turned forty the year before me. I couldn't wait to plan an event he would remember for a lifetime. Bill's good friend Steve Keuer was also about to go over the hill. His wife Debbie is a close friend of mine, so we planned an incredible birthday party for the two of them. We invited 150 people to a fun cruise-theme party with elaborate food, music, and decorations. It was a great party!

When my birthday rolled around, I wanted to make sure that Bill was planning a wonderful social event for me. As the day drew closer, I got nervous when I didn't notice anything going on behind the scenes to prepare for my party. I finally broke the silence on the topic and asked him point blank, "Bill, what kind of elaborate affair are you planning for my big day?"

"Well," he answered, "I was going to take you out for a special dinner—just the two of us." When the tears welled up in my eyes, we both knew it was time to talk.

Bill confessed to me that he loved the party I gave him, but what he really wanted was a wonderful night alone with me. I shared with him that I wanted the party I gave him to send the message for him to do it up big on *my* birthday. We both wanted to give each other what we selfishly wanted for ourselves—not what we thought the other person would like.

As it turned out, Bill was planning a wonderful surprise birthday party for me and sent beautiful invitations to a hundred of "my most intimate circle of friends," as he put it. Good food, good friends, and a string quartet made a memory I won't soon forget. For Bill's forty-first birthday, I took him to Dallas for an intimate evening for two at a hotel. So we both eventually got what we wanted. But once again we realized that we're in a life-long challenge to meet each other's needs . . . not to mention desires.

I hate to admit it but Bill is catching on to this principle faster than I am. Just last summer I fell into the same old habitual pattern of doing what I wanted to do instead of being sensitive to what Bill wanted. As Father's Day approached, he left a catalog conspicuously open on my desk with a picture of a 35mm zoom lens. How boring, I thought, to know what you're going to receive as a present on a special day. No way will I buy him a zoom lens. I'm going to buy him the surprise of his life. Boy will he be excited!

Knowing that he loves to fish, the boys and I made a trip to the sporting-goods store and bought Bill a fishing vest to rival any *Field and Stream* advertisement. When we presented it to him on Father's Day, he was, of course, excited about his vest. But he told me later that what he really wanted was a zoom lens. Once again I had imposed on him my love of surprise . . . and a surprise was the last thing he wanted. He tried to make that clear by leaving the catalog on my desk.

Bill, on the other hand, had been listening for clues to my desires and thus learned that I would someday like to have a string of pearls. As fine jewelry is not in our budget at this point in our lives (and probably never will be), I had designated this wish as a post-college-for-our-kids, late-life luxury. Because I keep all the checkbooks at my desk, I know what goes in and out of all the accounts. It's hard for Bill to ever buy anything without my knowing about it. So, he secretly stashed money for pearls in his sock drawer for a year. He saved over a thousand dollars in cash. When he gave me the pearls, I was dumbfounded—not only that he could get away with it without my finding out—but that he would plan this special surprise for me. I wondered if I would ever be as sensitive toward him.

Learning to live with a person who is diametrically different from you can be painfully stretching. There are many days when I would like to tightly wrap Bill's paisley tie around his neck. And I give Bill plenty of opportunities to want to strangle me with my pearls. Our differences cause us the deepest pain, but also the most intense joy. We certainly haven't "arrived" in our marriage by anyone's standard, but there are a few things we've learned over the past twenty-one years about loving and communicating with each other.

First, we must accept each other as unique creations of God and recognize that our personalities need enhancement, not alteration. Many women, including myself, said "I do" with a civilize-the-barbarian mentality. All this man needs is a woman's touch . . . I'll whip him into shape in no time, we secretly strategize.

Men have designs of their own too. As they envision their fantasies becoming reality, they think, Now she's mine, to meet my every need and fulfill my every desire . . . I've been waiting years for this. Rather than changing our mates into what we think they should be, we actually drive them even farther away from where we are trying to take them.

This means we need to stop criticizing each other. I'll never forget the day Bill told me he would strive to accept me like I am and never criticize me again. You'd think I would have been elated. Instead, I felt frustrated and even a little mad. If he stops criticizing me, I pondered silently, that means that I'll have to stop criticizing him . . . and how will he ever become the man he needs to be without my help?

After stewing for a few days, I realized that I needed to accept Bill "as is" as God's gift to me. We made that decision more than ten years ago, although I'm sorry to say we've both reneged more times than we care to make public. On the days when I lose chapters on my computer because I didn't save them in the right file, Bill is sure that I was born without a left hemisphere in my brain. "Why aren't you careful to save your work correctly? I've explained this to you a hundred times. I don't believe you really want to learn."

Then when he asks me for the fiftieth time if a tie goes with a certain shirt and sport coat, I am tempted to think the man not only has no taste in clothes, but is legally color-blind. "Why, for Pete's sake, do I have to continue to dress you after all these years? Is your taste only in your mouth? Can't you intuitively see that fabrics, patterns, and styles must be in harmony to look right?" Embarrassingly, the cutting words come all too easily when we forget our decision to stop the criticism and celebrate our differences. We often have to remind ourselves that neither one of us is perfect and God made us husband and wife to complement each other's strengths and weaknesses. We're a powerful team when we remember this.

Second, we must learn to say I love you in a way that communicates to the other person. God made us to like different things. Bill wants me to praise him sincerely in private. I, on the other hand, feel so proud when Bill compliments me in front of others and demonstrates his love openly for the world to see. So what do we find ourselves doing more times than we care to confess? He demonstrates his love to me privately, and I broadcast my adoration for him to anyone who will listen. It is hard for me to understand why this means nothing to him, when I can think of nothing I'd like better. Sometimes when we feel empty, we look at each other, shake our heads, and wonder if we'll ever learn to communicate our love to each other in a meaningful way.

Since the way we would like to be loved does not come naturally for either of us, we have to discipline ourselves to be sensitive about this. Bill tries to remember that I love an audience and I want the whole world to know he loves me. And I have to write notes to myself about showing Bill my love one-on-one. Otherwise I forget.

Third, we both must proactively look for things we enjoy in common. Because Bill and I are so different, we constantly try to find things we like to do together. We don't want to end up living in two separate worlds. Years ago we discovered that we both enjoy art and decided to start collecting paintings to fill the walls of our home. We began to purchase favorite works of art at places we visited on vacations. Now our home is filled with memories of these trips.

We've also learned we enjoy doing projects together that will enhance our home, such as upholstering, refinishing antiques, stripping and staining hardwood floors, laying tile, and remodeling a kitchen, to name a few. Working on a project together causes bonding to take place. And when we finish a job that we've labored on together, we feel so proud.

We've learned to give each other space for different interests as well. When we individually pursue various hobbies, friendships, and aspects of our careers, we become more interesting to each other as we share what we've experienced.

And fourth, we must give ourselves sacrificially to each other. Before we were married, no request was too big, no chore was a bother, no favor was too much trouble. We couldn't do enough for each other. But when the newness of marital bliss began to run thin, so did our patience.

One day Bill and I jokingly wrote The Six Stages of Marital Cooperation. Although we wrote it to be humorous, we confess that the words ring truer than either of us is comfortable acknowledging.

First year: "Lovey-dovey, I know you've got that big project due today. I want to do everything I can to help. Your problem is my problem. We're in this together! I'll put this little bell in your office and you just ring if you need anything. I'll be there in a jiffy. I'll take care of dinner and fix your favorite dessert."

Second year: "Listen, Hon, don't you have a project due soon? Let me lock you in your room and I'll try not to disturb you. I'll bring you a sandwich about six o'clock."

Third year: "Hey, Babe, sorry I'm in a hurry. I forgot all about your big deadline. Here's a twenty. Why don't you order in pizza for dinner?"

Fourth year: "Look, Dear, I know you've got this project, but I've scheduled a big meeting tonight. You're on your own for dinner."

Fifth year: "If you'd just plan ahead you wouldn't get yourself in these last-minute crunches."

Sixth year: "I can't believe you've done this again! There are other people with lives in this house! I needed *you* to fix dinner tonight."

The bottom line is that marriage takes time and commitment, two commodities we always seem to be short on. Quite frankly, I got married with a Ward and June Cleaver outlook—that we'd have two children, a yard with a picket fence, and a dog. And as a good mom, I'd wear a shirt-waist dress and apron and wave good-bye to my family each morning before beginning my household chores. Each night our family would eat dinner together in the dining room. Any problems we encountered could be worked out in thirty minutes.

It didn't take long for reality to set in. With our calendars filled with work, kids' activities, community projects, and church meetings, some days we feel we're scheduled up to eternity. Stressed out and living on a fast track, it's hard to spend any quality time together as husband and wife.

We often get dangerously close to the crash-and-burn stage in our marriage before we realize we're desperate. It is then that we step back, take stock of the situation, and remind ourselves that a good marriage doesn't just happen. It takes not only time, but a lot of work, patience, and prayer. When we let our relationship deteriorate to a place where we endure instead of enjoy each other, commitment not to bale out is sometimes the only thing we have to hang on to. I'm convinced though, that God doesn't want us just to tolerate each other, but desires for us to have a rich and fulfilling relationship. With his help this can happen.

In 1 Peter 3:8–12 Bill and I found guidelines that we strive to apply to our marriage. There are plenty of days when we want to do just the opposite than what the passage says, but we're committed to make this our goal.

". . . live in harmony with one another; be sympathetic, love as brothers, be compassionate and humble. Do not repay evil with evil or insult with insult, but with blessing, because to this you were called so that you may inherit a blessing. For,

> 'Whoever would love life
>> and see good days
> must keep his tongue from evil
>> and his lips from deceitful speech.
> He must turn from evil and do good;
>> he must seek peace and pursue it.
> For the eyes of the Lord are on the righteous
>> and his ears are attentive to their prayer,
> but the face of the Lord is against those who
>> do evil.'"

Daily Disciplines

"There is no more lovely, friendly, and charming relationship, communion or company than a good marriage"—Martin Luther.

There's probably not a couple in the world who entered marriage thinking, No way will this marriage work. Our goal is to make each other miserable. But somewhere along the way we realize that if it is going to work, it's going to take some work. And after a few years we see that if we're going to enjoy rather than endure each other, something's got to change—and it's usually me.

A good marriage is worth every ounce of energy it takes to fight for it. And it's a daily battle. The following list of daily disciplines comes from our twenty-one-year saga of victories and defeats. Although many of the battles have been bitter, there's nothing sweeter than the communion we've enjoyed when they're over.

You'll know what works in your relationship. As you read the following disciplines, jot down ideas you can apply to your marriage—then act upon them.

- Remember, love is a verb. Act on it every day. Take time to say, "I love you." Do some little thing for your husband. Pay attention to his true heart's desire.

- Get away together without the kids—even if it's only for a couple of days—at least twice a year.

- Tackle a new project together. Buy a piece of antique furniture and refinish it together. It will not only be something to enhance your home, but it will hold fond memories of the time you spent together working on it. In twenty-one years of marriage we've bought only three pieces of new furniture. The other "early-attic" pieces each have a memory attached to them, such as the oak buffet we bought for seventy-five dollars, the thirty-five-dollar den chair we stayed up until four o'clock upholstering, and our kitchen table and chairs that Bill painted when I was pregnant with Joel. Be creative. If your first ideas for joint projects don't work out, try something else. The real failure is failing to connect, not failing to finish a project.

❦ Subscribe to a magazine you both enjoy and read it together. Bill and I look forward to staying up after the kids go to bed and looking through *Southern Living* once a month together.

❦ Respect your mate's privacy. Don't open each other's mail.

❦ Set aside some time to meet over coffee and discuss your family goals.

❦ Take a class together and learn something new. We enjoyed taking ballroom dancing.

❦ Display your wedding pictures in your home. Talk about how you fell in love. Tell your children too.

❦ Never go to bed angry. On the nights I rebel against this principle, I always regret it the next day.

❦ Sit down together at the first of each month and look over your calendars and schedules. We've wasted a lot of emotional energy getting upset over missed or double-booked events and appointments.

❦ Listen to tapes together when you go on short trips in the car. Talk about what you learn.

❦ Attend a marriage-enrichment retreat once a year.

❦ Set aside time to pray together regularly. We've learned we have to be sensitive to each other's preferences—even about prayer. Bill likes to pray from a list in a structured manner, making sure all points are covered in a methodical way. I like to be more spontaneous. Neither way is spiritually right or wrong.

❦ Cut your mate some slack. We all have eccentricities.

❦ Introduce your spouse to a new book or author. Bill and I discovered that we both enjoy historical novels by George MacDonald. It's fun to talk about the characters, setting, and plot after we've both read the book.

❦ Set a goal to live your lives in such a way as to help each other do the will of God.

❦ "Keep your eyes wide open before marriage, half shut afterwards"—Benjamin Franklin. Is there something bothering you about your husband? Are you being picky? If you're not sure, ask yourself the question, "Do I want him to judge me in the same way I'm judging him?"

❦ Take walks together. One couple takes a brisk three-mile walk in forty-five minutes every morning. This is their "talk time."

❦ "A gentle answer turns away wrath, but a harsh word stirs up anger" (Prov. 15:1). Words cannot be retracted. When you're having a conflict with your husband, silently say a prayer and ask God to help you respond wisely.

❧ Encourage your mate to go on outings and trips with friends. Send your husband on a hunting or fishing trip with the guys, and ask him to keep the kids while you go on a retreat with the girls. You'll both come home refreshed.

❧ Make a list of ways you like for your husband to tell you he loves you. Ask him to do the same. Exchange lists and review them regularly. Then put them into action.

❧ Take time out for yourself. You can't connect with your mate when you're tired and on edge.

❧ Go out on dates often.

❧ Realize that your mate will never be able to meet all your needs. God has promised to do that.

❧ Encourage each other to do new things alone as well as together. Take a class. Then come back and share what you learned.

❧ Start a dinner club with friends that you both enjoy. It will enhance your relationship to have "our" friends, in addition to "yours" and "mine."

❧ Attend a Bible study with your spouse, or host one in your home. Grow spiritually together.

❧ Pray this prayer for your marriage: "Grant that we may not so much seek to be understood as to understand"—Saint Francis of Assisi.

❦ Don't give each other lectures or sermons. Nobody needs another parent or Holy Spirit.

❦ See your pastor or a good Christian counselor to help you sort through problems that seem impossible to solve. Don't give up.

❦ Compliment your spouse often.

❦ "Marriage resembles a pair of shears, so joined that they can not be separated; often moving in opposite directions, yet always punishing anyone who comes between them"—Sydney Smith. Can you relate to this?

❦ Never criticize your mate in front of others.

❦ Write your husband a letter if you feel uncomfortable verbalizing your feelings. When you fight, fight fair. Bill and I are still trying to learn to listen actively to what the other is saying. It's hard to just acknowledge and listen without reacting.

❦ "Once a word has been allowed to escape, it cannot be recalled"—Horace. Ask God to help you choose your words carefully when you express your feelings.

❦ Help each other reach a personal goal, such as continuing an educational pursuit or learning a new skill.

❦ Send funny cards with loving messages to your spouse's office.

❦ Be actively interested in each other's world.

❦ "One's best asset is a sympathetic spouse"— Euripides. Does this describe you?

Self-Disciplines

❦ Have any of the stories from this chapter hit home in your relationship? Try to think of some funny misunderstandings from your marriage. Laugh about them with your husband. And on days when the communication channels seem clogged in your relationship, glance over the ideas in this chapter. Try one thing that feels comfortable to get the words and feelings flowing again.

Part 3

Confessions of a
Desperate Mother

7

I Was the Perfect Mother—But I Got Over It

I've often wondered why children don't come with a warning label. When we brought our first child home from the hospital, I didn't know I had committed myself for the next twelve months to functioning in a state somewhere between comatose and catatonic. Neither did I realize that I'd signed over my rights to carry on an uninterrupted adult conversation for the next eighteen years.

In the last trimester of my pregnancy, I fantasized about our new family. In my dream I was, of course, the perfect mother. Our home was spotless and smelled of baby lotion. Dressed in a beautiful Pima cotton gown and robe, I rocked our infant who lay quietly bundled in lacy blankets. Every hair on my head was perfectly arranged and my makeup flawless. I had already lost the fifty-five pounds I managed to gain in eight months. And Bill stood by my side, hand-feeding me grapes and gourmet crackers.

Talk about rude awakenings. First of all, the aroma that permeated our house gave new meaning to the word asphyxiation. I wondered why baby stores don't sell gas masks. And after twenty-four hours of nonstop infant discharge from both ends, I didn't own a clean item of clothing. Surely I could sell the research rights to the stains I couldn't identify. Why didn't disposable diaper ads show parents dodging projectile diarrhea? As for my hair and makeup, my new look protected me from all door-to-door salesmen. They ran when I answered the door. And Bill told me not to worry about the fifty-five pounds. He was sure I still had time to qualify for the trained whale show. (He was just trying to kid me out of the doldrums, but I didn't think it was a laughing matter.)

It took about a week for us to throw out any preconceived philosophies we once held about family life. Our home was out of control. But I'm a proud person, and I wanted the outside world to think that universities were funding programs to study our astute parenting skills. Early on we tried to impress our friends with our shrewd tactics.

I announced one night at a dinner party that Bill and I had made an important decision: Not a drop of anything foreign would touch our child's lips—I planned to nurse for three years. It only took eight months and two jars of nipple balm to figure out that teething babies aren't exactly user-friendly.

As our first-born grew up we continued to use a trial-and-error method—mostly error—to formulate our parenting strategy. High on our list of priorities we listed good nutrition, believing that a healthy family is a happy family—which may be true in some cases. (It had the opposite effect on ours.)

I got into this nutritional thing in a big way. I decided with fervor, "Not a granule of white sugar or refined flour will pass our threshold again." I drove to a farm to buy honey straight from the hive, bought undefiled peanut butter for fifteen dollars a jar, stocked up on organic rice cakes, and baked homemade bread—which we could have used for a doorstop.

Every morning I self-righteously prepared a healthy lunch for my first-grader. I turned up my nose at less conscientious mothers who actually put chips and cup-cakes in their children's lunches. How irresponsible, I thought smugly.

When it came time for my parent-teacher conference, the teacher assured me that John was doing very well in school. But she questioned my attitude toward nutrition. "Did you know, Mrs. Peel, that your son eats donuts and candy bars every day for lunch?" It seems that by noon, John's sandwich had turned into a ball of mush. And the kids used my cookies for Frisbees on the playground. The other children felt sorry for John, so they took turns do-nating their extras to him every day. The Rice Cake Era of our family ended—suddenly. And, to tell the truth, I was relieved. I'm still not a very good cook. And, while we try to limit sweets and junk foods, I realized that I'd gone overboard—when it was really my bread that should have. It would have made the perfect anchor.

Most parents struggle with disengaging their self-es-teem from the behavior of their children, but I was a hard case. I came by this predisposition honestly. My mother dressed me to perfection every time I went out the door. So, of course my children had to look their best as well. Growing up in an all-girl family, I had no appreciation for the proper attire for boy's play. When Bill questioned why John had to wear polished saddle oxfords to play in the sandbox, I had an excellent reason: "You should al-ways look your best. Other people treat you better when you are dressed well." Actually, I confess I was more con-cerned about how others perceived and treated me than how they treated my child. It also did not occur to me that a five-year-old boy on the playground in a sailor suit might be considered sissy—and fights could ensue.

I also expected my children to be perfect specimens of humanity in public, which, of course, they were not. (I have since decided that this approach to determining my self-worth ranks somewhere between harebrained and demented.) They were always on display no matter what we were doing.

When Bill asked if we could have a dinner party for the people in one of his Bible studies, I responded, "Sure, Honey, that would be a wonderful gesture of hospitality." I was actually thinking, Now's my chance to show off our wonderful Christian children. When these people leave our home, they will think our family is God's gift to Tyler, Texas.

I addressed invitations to twenty-four people for a formal seated dinner. That was my first mistake since I enjoy cooking about as much as I enjoy filing our income tax. My second mistake was not sending the children to Grandma's for the evening. With my perfectionist attitude, I was a sitting duck for disaster.

The guests were asked to arrive by 7:30. At 7:20, Joel wobbled into the family room acting very strangely. We began asking him questions and looking in every room for clues to his unusual behavior. We found the evidence in the bathroom—an open bottle of mouthwash on the counter. It was nearly empty.

Remembering the main ingredient in mouthwash is alcohol, we understood why Joel couldn't walk a straight line: our three-year-old was drunk. We called our pediatrician immediately. He told us to put him in a cold shower, then let him sleep it off in bed. Hopefully he wouldn't have a hangover the next day.

I propped our tipsy toddler up against the shower wall, and Bill answered the doorbell. Fortunately, of the first four guests to arrive, two were physicians with a sense of humor. They calmed us down by trying to help us see the comedy of the situation. They monitored Joel during the evening, and the dinner party came off without another hitch. He woke up the morning and never knew what happened. Today we laugh about this as a family.

You would think after this embarrassing episode, I would have learned my lesson. But it seems that more times than not, God must teach me the same principles over and over. In late summer of 1990, *A Mother's Manual for Schoolday Survival* was released. It was a thrill to have our book featured on the cover of the September issue of *Focus on the Family* magazine, which has a circulation of two million families. My pride began to swell. Isn't God honored to have me as his "spokesmom"? I thought conceitedly. In my pride, I knew if I claimed to have helpful answers for busy mothers, my children had best be examples of what I write about. I selfishly hoped they would have a good year in school—for my benefit as well as theirs.

The second week of school our radio program with Dr. James Dobson aired. Driving to school that day to pick up James from kindergarten, I beamed as I listened to the tape of our broadcast. Kathy, how do you do it? I smiled and complimented myself in the rear-view mirror. But as I pulled into the school driveway and saw the look on James's face, as well as the teacher's, I turned off the radio.

"Kathy, we need to talk," she whispered seriously. James began to cry. She related to me how James punched another boy in the stomach at recess, and that was grounds for school discipline. Hoping she didn't know I was on the radio that day, I thanked her and told her I would deal with the problem. Deflated, I drove home.

The two-minute drive home seemed like two hours. I asked James to go to his room so we could talk. Sitting on the edge of his bed, I began the inquisition.

"James, did you punch Tommy in the stomach today?" I asked.

"Yes, ma'am," he replied quietly.

"Where did you learn to punch someone in the stomach? Have you ever seen Mommy punch Daddy in the stomach?" I continued the questioning. My voice was not getting calmer.

"No, ma'am."

"Have you ever seen your brothers punch anyone in the stomach?" my voice grew impatient.

"No, ma'am."

"Then *why*, for the love of peace, did you do this?" I finished ungraciously.

"Well," he looked at me seriously, "Tommy wouldn't stop bugging me. I asked him to stop, but he wouldn't. He made me so mad I just felt like socking him. I'm sorry, Mommy."

His honesty touched my heart. You know, I thought empathetically, there are times when people make me so mad I feel like punching them in the stomach. I also knew that if God was not gracious and forgiving, he would probably like to punch *me* in the stomach regularly for my obnoxious behavior. I hugged James with compassion.

I helped him call the little boy he hit so he could apologize. That night Bill and I talked to all three boys about correct and incorrect ways to handle our inevitable feelings of anger. This event turned into a learning experience for us all. But I needed it more than anyone. I saw once more how I put too much pressure on my kids to perform. I asked God again to help me get through this stage so I could give my kids the freedom to fail that he daily gives me.

I have always heard the old adage that about the time your kids stop embarrassing you, you start embarrassing them. This could never be true of me, I thought with confidence. I'll just look cool, act cool, and they'll think I'm cool.

I'm smart enough to know the first prerequisite of getting the approval of teenagers is making sure you don't look like a "geek." Before a recent family ski trip I asked a cute college girl at the sporting goods store to show me the latest styles for the slopes. I didn't want the guys to be embarrassed to ski with me. She led me to a rack of stretch pants.

I need to pause here and tell you what I think about women who look good in stretch pants. I hate them. The way I see it, if God had wanted women to wear stretch pants he wouldn't have given some of us industrial-size thighs. Nor would any of us be under six feet tall.

After pouring myself into the stretch pants, I wondered how long I could go without breathing. I felt like a giant Jell-O mold. "Oh, you look fabulous, Mrs. Peel," she lied. "Just let me find you a long colorful jacket." (Meaning: Let's cover up your bulging thighs so you won't be laughed off the slopes.)

We finally pulled together a perfectly coordinated ski look to the tune of $257. But what's money when you're going to make great memories with your kids?

My goal for our first day on the slopes was not to fall down. I knew that would embarrass the kids. (I'm considering going for counseling to get to the root cause of why I tend consistently to set unreachable goals for myself.) I should have known it was going to be a long day when a man asked me which way to the children's ski school and I fell flat on my face in front of him. I didn't have my skis on yet.

After standing in line to get on the ski lift for the first run of the day, I tried really hard to get on unobtrusively. I sat down smoothly, but when I looked back to see if the guys had made it on, I realized that Joel had dropped a ski. At that point I did what any nurturing, caring mother would do. I jumped off the ski lift to help. My children looked the other way when I landed in a pile of snow—ski tips pointing skyward.

"Mom, we don't know you," they whispered as their chair moved over the scene of my accident. "That was probably not your most intelligent move."

We finally rendezvoused at the top of the mountain and began our descent. When I arrived at the bottom ten minutes behind them, they asked if there might be another sport for "older" people that I might enjoy more.

Our kids, aged eighteen, fourteen, and seven, are amazingly well-adjusted—considering all of the insecurities and developmental stages they've had to take their parents through. Actually, I think that's probably the big problem with most child-raising philosophies. It's the child who should say to the parent, "Don't worry. You'll get over this. You're just going through a stage."

We sat down with our older boys one night and asked what they thought children would want parents to know about raising them. Together we came up with the following guidelines for parents:

The Ten Biggies: Teenage Wisdom
for Today's Parents

1. I'm the only me there is here. Accept and respect my differences. Affirm me regularly. Treat me with courtesy.

2. Show me the behaviors you want me to follow. I want to do as you do, not as you say.

3. When you're wrong, admit it. I'm sorry may be the second most important thing you can say to me. I love you is the first.

4. Trust me. When you think highly of me, I want to live up to your expectations.

5. Set limits and stick to them. You can be a firm parent and still be a fun parent.

6. Give me the freedom to fail. When I make a bad decision and suffer the consequences, stand by me. Let me know you still love me, although you disapprove of what I did.

7. Be interested in my world. I spell love T-I-M-E. Let's do things together—things I like and you like too. Spend time doing fun things with me regularly.

8. Be a good listener. Try to respond wisely, not react impulsively to what I share with you. I want to know you'll always hear me out.

9. Don't go for the neatest house in the neighborhood award. Let me be a little messy. My projects create some chaos.

10. Don't sweat the small stuff. A forgotten homework assignment doesn't carry the same weight as finding drugs in my drawer. Save your steam for the majors, and don't come down too hard on the minors. Be consistent.

(Note: It's important for parents to stand together on what they feel are the behavioral big deals. Spend time alone with your spouse and talk about this issue. Our "big deals" are sex, drugs, alcohol, dishonesty, and disrespect for authority.)

I have to pray regularly that God will help me remember these guidelines and apply them to daily happenings. It's also important to pray for and with our children. Once when I was speaking in Dallas on the topic of motherhood, a young mom walked up to me and said, "I want to pray with my children every night, but I have to confess—'Now I lay me down to sleep' is getting a little old. Is there anything else I can pray?"

I can remember feeling this way as a young mother—wanting to pray in a meaningful way—but not knowing exactly how. Over the years I have developed patterns that—although are certainly not straight from Mount Sinai—I feel are in harmony with how God would want me to pray with and for my children.

When praying with them, I use a simple three-part prayer procedure. It includes specific thanksgiving, confirmation, and requests that they can understand. The prayer can be as long or as short as time allows. A typical prayer with my seven-year-old goes something like this:

> Thank you, Father, that you are right here with us every moment, and you care about everything in our lives. Thank you that we can lay here in a comfortable bed with warm covers and a soft pillow. You take such good care of us and give us everything we need plus a lot of things we want.
>
> Thank you for allowing James to be a member of our family and for letting me be his mommy. James is such a special boy. He is kind, honest, helpful, and a good friend to others. He shares his toys and plays fair.

(Note: On the days when James is unkind, stingy with his toys, or gets a spanking for telling a lie, I feel like I have to stretch the truth to state these positive characteristics. But since God treats me this way, I use this as a model for how I deal with my children. On the days when I'm unkind, stingy with my possessions, or deceitful, God tells me that I am holy and blameless [see Eph. 1:4]. This motivates me to strive to live up to what he says I really am. As James hears me pray and confirm positive qualities in his life, he begins to see himself in that way and wants to practice those behaviors.)

> Father, you know that James has a spelling test tomorrow. I ask that you help him think clearly and remember his words. I also ask that you help Grandma feel better.

Protect us from evil and harm and help us to obey what we know you would want us to do. In Jesus' name we pray. Amen.

When I pray for my children, I write in my prayer journal requests based on Scripture. I've made lists and notes in my Bible of characteristics I know God would want to build into my children's lives. Once again, it can be a short prayer based on a verse or two, or you may want to personalize and pray an entire chapter for your children. (The possibilities are almost endless.) Use the following verses to stimulate your thinking about what to pray:

Father, I thank you for John, Joel, and James. They are truly a blessing from you (Ps. 127:3). For each of them I pray:

that their hearts would be open to receive your wisdom and discipline, that they might acquire a disciplined and prudent life, and do what is right and just and fair (Prov. 1:2–3).

that they would see danger and take refuge (Prov. 22:3).

that they would have great peace and love your law, and nothing would make them stumble (Ps. 119:165).

that they would learn to not pay back wrong for wrong, but always try to be kind to each other and to everyone else (1 Thess. 5:15).

And Father, I pray that you would help Bill and me not exasperate the boys, but bring them up in your training and instruction (Eph. 6:4).

You will want to develop your own method of expressing your desires for your children to God. Remember it's okay to feel awkward or uncomfortable. He understands. All he asks for is a sincere heart.

There are many times when I feel so desperate for
his answers and his help, I don't even know where to begin.
It is then that I find great comfort in Romans 8:26–27:

> In the same way, the Spirit helps us in our weakness.
> We do not know what we ought to pray for, but the Spirit
> himself intercedes for us with groans that words cannot
> express. And he who searches our hearts knows the mind
> of the Spirit, because the Spirit intercedes for the saints in
> accordance with God's will.

Although I entered motherhood rather flippantly,
through the years I've come to see my role not only as a big
responsibility, but also a great privilege. I've found that the
greatest child-raising philosopher and mentor of all time
is my Heavenly Father. As he lovingly deals with me as
his child, he teaches me how to parent my children. I've
learned to evaluate any parenting philosophy by asking
the simple question, "Is this how my Heavenly Father deals
with me?" Four important principles stand out to me.

The Principle of Success

Perhaps the most important principle I've learned is
a new way to measure my success as a parent. It is easy
for me to look for my personal sense of well-being from my
child's behavior. This has always led me to a strategy of
control and manipulation. In the guise of responsible
parenting, I destroy not only my child's self-worth but our
relationship for the temporary pleasure of seeing him act
in a way that reflects well on me. I'll never forget the embarrassment and frustration I felt when two-year-old John
pitched a fit in the grocery store. I pushed my cart behind
the potato chip stand and angrily gave him a swat. Although
his behavior needed to be dealt with, my attitude was
entirely selfish. I was more concerned with how the store

full of shoppers viewed John's behavior as a reflection of my parental prowess than how to discipline his actions wisely.

Although I tried to get away with overcontrol when the kids were young, the day came when I realized this was not only impossible, but foolish and unbiblical. This is not how God treats me. He gives me real choices with real consequences. He does not rate his success on my behavior but his. In the same way, he doesn't hold me responsible for whether my children turn out right, but for being the right kind of parent. I need to focus my attention on my performance as a parent, not on what my children are doing. I am not responsible for what I get out of my children, only what I put into them. This has given me a great deal of freedom when they don't have the highest grades in the class or behave with the proper manners or exhibit Christlike attitudes. I can focus on what they need and what is best for them, whether it is discipline, love, instruction, rebuke, or simply a swat on the bottom.

A friend shared with me that he has never felt close to his mother because of the stringent expectations she put on him as a five-year-old. "Your behavior is a reflection on our family. You're the pastor's son, and everyone is watching you. When you misbehave, you're an embarrassment to your father and me." These were harsh words to the ears of a young child, and as a middle-aged man he can still hear the controlling tone in her voice. Should the career success of parents rest on the shoulders of a child? As horrible as this sounds, we will all succumb to this kind of manipulation when we evaluate our success by our children's behavior.

The Principle of Focus

While I cannot control what my child becomes, my desire is not just for outward conformity, but inner change.

My Heavenly Father is interested in much more than my behavior. He is interested in my heart—mind, will, and emotions. Christ rebuked the Jews when he said of them, "These people honor me with their lips, but their hearts are far from me" (Matt. 15:8). As a parent, daily dealing with outward obedience is not optional, but I need to always keep in mind the need for inner growth as well. I am a partner with God in building character into the lives of my children. Since our kids are growing up in a world that bombards them daily with blatantly sinful philosophies, it is important that we regularly and naturally present truth to their growing intellect, heart, and conscience. Moses gave parents great advice when he instructed Israel:

"Love the Lord your God with all your heart and with all your soul and with all your strength. These commandments that I give you today are to be upon your hearts. Impress them on your children. Talk about them when you sit at home and when you walk along the road, when you lie down and when you get up. Tie them as symbols on your hands and bind them on your foreheads. Write them on the doorframes of your houses and on your gates" (Deut. 6:5–9).

Over the years we have had various structured family devotional times. These times are good—and important—but we think the most meaningful spiritual learning experiences have occurred during the daily routines of life. When the kids receive extra money in change at a store, or when it would be easy for them to state references on a paper that really weren't used, we talk about the importance of honesty. When Bill or I get impatient, critical, or angry, it's good for the kids to see us acknowledge and confess our behavior to those we've offended. It is a perfect time to talk about our sin and God's forgiveness. When we enjoy a beautiful sunset or go mountain climbing as a family, this is a natural time to praise God for his creative power and grandeur.

The Principle of Attraction

The basis of my relationship with my Heavenly Father is his unconditional love for me, not my behavior. I am drawn to obedience not because of fear of retribution, but out of a desire to please my God who loves me so passionately. Although I consistently let him down and abuse his trust in me, he still claims me as his own.

If I want my children to accept my values, they must know how much I value them. Years ago Bill Kraftson, a friend with Search Ministries, taught me one of the most important principles of evangelism. "People don't care how much we know until they know how much we care." This isn't just a principle for evangelism. It is a principle for life—especially parenting. Children are attracted, not indoctrinated, to biblical values. All my instructions, all the Sunday school lessons, and all of our family Bible reading will fall on hard hearts, if they are not softened by our unconditional love and the knowledge that we believe in them. A friend's story illustrates this well.

When seventeen-year-old Suzie skipped two monthly periods, her mother, Mary Ann, made an appointment at the gynecologist to investigate the problem. The doctor administered a pregnancy test and the results came back positive. Mary Ann and her husband loved their children and had always taught them the value of sexual purity. They were understandably devastated by the news. When Mary Ann asked Suzie about her relationship with her steady boyfriend, Suzie adamantly responded that they had never had any kind of intimate physical contact. Although the evidence looked otherwise, Mary Ann chose to trust her daughter's word. Under extreme protest from the doctor, they asked for another pregnancy test to be run. This time the test came back negative. Mary Ann was not only relieved, but thankful she had believed in her daughter. This incident strengthened even more the love and respect between this mother and daughter.

The Principle of Individuality

My Heavenly Father always treats me as an individual, never squeezing me into a mold. I have my own unique expression of my being. God delights in the diversity of his creatures rather than trying to make them all the same. I honor him and delight him when I seek to be the unique creature he made me to be. As my creator, he is the resident expert on my design, and works to help me develop what I am, not what I am not. As a parent, one of my first responsibilities is to understand the detailed uniqueness of each of my boys. One size does not fit all in the realm of parenting styles. Each boy requires different help, encouragement, discipline, nurture, and a different teaching style. Just as God customizes his style to fit the way he made me, I must adjust my parenting style with each child. I wish I had known this when John was young.

In my early years of motherhood I made the mistake of looking to everyone else but my child to decide what were the right things to do. Since most every other four-year-old played soccer, I signed John up for soccer. He never really liked soccer, and we spent a lot of miserable Saturday mornings running up and down the soccer field. Because all supposedly well-rounded children played a musical instrument, I enrolled him in preschool music school at a local university and private piano lessons. Many an afternoon was ruined as he tried to like this pursuit so important to his mother. "And why," I worried, "is he so content to spend hours alone creating and building new Lego designs, when he should be playing with lots of other boys his age? After all, I like to be surrounded by people. Why shouldn't he?" I didn't understand at the time I was trying to make him into something foreign to the way God created him. It was like forcing a square peg into a round hole.

As God tenderly and patiently taught me to rejoice in my own uniqueness, I began to transfer this philosophy to my children. I began to see myself more as a farmer than an architect. In their book *Discovering Your Child's Design,* Ralph Mattson and Thom Black develop this excellent analogy. A farmer cultivates and nurtures what is already resident within the seed. An architect creates a new design of his own fancy. We give lip service to the fact that children are so different, but our children come with intricate designs. They arrive in our homes with gifts of strength and motivations that God has placed in each of them according to his purpose. These uniquenesses must be honored not only for the child's sake but for our relationship with God. When we usurp the role of the architect from God, we devastate our children and place a barrier between us and our Father.

In the book *Growing Strong in the Seasons of Life* by Chuck Swindoll, I read a parable called "A Rabbit on the Swim Team." I think it illustrates the point well.

Once upon a time, the animals decided they should do something meaningful to meet the problems of the new world. So they organized a school.

They adopted an activity curriculum of running, climbing, swimming and flying. To make it easier to administer the curriculum, all the animals took all the subjects.

The *duck* was excellent in swimming; in fact, better than his instructor. But he made only passing grades in flying, and was very poor in running. Since he was slow in running, he had to drop swimming and stay after school to practice running. This caused his webbed feet to be badly worn, so that he was only average in swimming. But average was acceptable, so nobody worried about that—except the duck.

The *rabbit* started at the top of his class in running, but developed a nervous twitch in his muscles because of so much make-up work in swimming.

The *squirrel* was excellent in climbing, but he encountered constant frustration in flying class because his teacher made him start from the ground up instead of from the treetop down. He developed "charlie horses" from overexertion, and so only got a C in climbing and a D in running.

The *eagle* was a problem child and was severely disciplined for being a nonconformist. In climbing classes he beat all the others to the top of the tree, but insisted on using his own way to get there . . .

I don't want to cripple my children like this, but I do when I don't honor their design. Striving to be a good mother is just one more area in my life where I daily feel desperate for God's help. I'm thankful all I have to do is ask for his wisdom and he gives it to me freely (James 1:5).

When our children were young, Bill and I scheduled a series of breakfast dates to talk about the character qualities we wanted to strive to build into our children and what values we wanted them to understand when they left home. We wrote the following list of life guidelines from Scripture feeling it our responsibility to teach them to our children, but knowing it is their choice whether or not they choose to embrace them.

The Teach-Your-Children-Well List

❦ The Lord, the first person of the universe, should be the first person of my life (Col. 1:17–18).

❦ The person who knows how to pray is the mightiest person in all the earth (Jer. 33:3).

❦ Sin is a compulsion for the non-Christian, but a choice for the Christian (Rom. 6:1–11).

❦ What I feed my mind will determine what I think. How I think will determine how I live (Prov. 23:7).

❦ Don't look for satisfaction in money and possessions. Only the man who hungers after righteousness will be satisfied (Matt. 6:19–34).

❦ God provides all our needs: if I don't have it, I don't need it (Phil. 4:19).

❦ Contentment is more a matter of attitude than accumulation (Phil. 4:10–13).

❦ I am a unique piece of art created by the greatest Master (Eph. 2:10).

❦ Life is like a tapestry. Many times we see only the backside with all the knots, scrambled threads, and loose ends, but we can be sure God is producing a work of art (Rom. 8:28–29).

❦ I can't control my circumstances, but I can control my actions and my attitudes (2 Cor. 4:8–9).

❦ Your body belongs to God. Treat it and everyone else's with dignity and honor deserving of God's possession (1 Cor. 6:19–20).

❦ The most important human relationship I will establish is with my mate. It is for keeps. Take time. Do it carefully (Eph. 5:21–33).

❦ God has put you where you are for a purpose. "Bloom where you are planted" (see Phil. 1:12–14).

❦ Work is a gift of God. Discover what you love to do and do it with all your heart (Eccles. 5:19).

❦ There is no sacred or secular work, only sacred and secular attitudes (Col. 3:23—4:1).

❦ Be productive. "Make all you can. Save all you can. Give all you can"—John Wesley.

❦ Clinging to one's importance is the quickest way to lose it (Prov. 16:18).

❦ Words without actions are useless (Matt. 15:8).

Daily Disciplines

"Train a child in the way he should go, and when he is old he will not turn from it" (Prov. 22:6).

There are many days I feel desperate because the responsibilities of motherhood often seem overwhelming. I've often wondered why the law requires that we have a license to drive a car, catch fish, cut hair, and polish fingernails—but we don't need a license to become a mother. It's reassuring to know that although the job is bigger than I can ever handle alone, I don't have to do it alone. God is with me every step of the way.

When I feel disappointed because I've looked for my personal sense of well-being from my child's behavior, God reminds me to focus my attention on my performance as a parent, not on what my children are doing. When I cannot control what my child becomes outwardly, I remember God is interested in what he becomes inwardly. If I want my children to accept my values, God helps me lovingly to show them how I care—so they will care about what I know. And when I am tempted to squeeze a child into a mold of my choosing, God reminds me he uniquely created each boy and shows me ways to develop what he is, not what he is not.

I invite you to use the following expressions to get to know your children better, to focus on what's important to them, and to become an attractive force in their lives. God will teach you to do this. All you have to do is ask. And as we learn how to love and care for our children, we learn how to be better children of God, our Father.

- ❦ "It is a wise father that knows his own child"—Shakespeare. Set aside some time daily just to listen to your child and enter into his or her world.

- ❦ Be a student of your child. Begin a journal recording your observations. Make a list of the activities you know your child enjoys (WARNING! Not what you enjoy or you enjoy him or her doing). If your child is older, you can ask him to list what he enjoys. Then ask the following questions:

    What seems to get him/her started in this activity?

    What does he/she enjoy accomplishing?

    Where did the activity take place?

    How does he/she do it?

    Are there other people involved? What are they doing?

    What materials, things, data, or ideas does he/she need?

    Wherever you see consistency, you have uncovered a part of his/her design.

❦ Take time to consider the following:

> Where do my design and my child's design clash?

> How well does his/her learning environment fit his/her design?

❦ Take a good look at how you criticize your child. If it is from a controlling or manipulative position, then ask your child to forgive you.

❦ "Example is not the main thing in influencing others. It is the only thing"—Albert Schweitzer. Set a good example for your children.

❦ Do your children think you are a fun person to be with? Be honest. You may need to loosen up a little and have some fun.

❦ "Before I formed you in the womb I knew you, before you were born I set you apart" (Jer. 1:5). Remind your child of this.

❦ Take a lot of pictures of your children. Display them throughout your house. Let them know you're proud to be their mom.

❦ "For you created my inmost being; you knit me together in my mother's womb. I praise you because I am fearfully and wonderfully made; your works are wonderful, I know that full well" (Ps. 139:13–14). Talk with your children about their unique qualities. Let them know they are a one-of-a-kind work of art.

❦ Make a big deal out of your kids' accomplishments and the things that are important in their world. Celebrate a report card that shows even the smallest progress. Fix a special meal to reward hard work on a science fair project—even if it didn't win. Display their artwork.

❦ Were you reared by an architect parent who tried to make you into something you maybe weren't, or a farmer parent who nurtured you and let you grow? How has this affected you?

❦ Schedule some time regularly to do something fun with each of your children. Make sure it's something the child wants to do.

❦ Praise your child for something every day.

❦ "Fathers, do not exasperate your children; instead, bring them up in the training and instruction of the Lord" (Eph. 6:4).

❦ Read *Train Up a Child,* by Rolf Zettersten.

❦ When was the last time you said I'm sorry to your child?

❦ Daily pray with and for your children.

❦ "My mother said to me, 'If you become a soldier you'll be a general; if you become a monk you'll end up as the pope.' Instead, I became a painter and wound up Picasso"—Pablo Picasso. Help your children dream big dreams about themselves.

❦ "Whatever you do, put romance and enthusiasm into the life of our children"—Margaret Ramsey MacDonald.

❦ Read the book *The Blessing,* by Gary Smalley and John Trent.

❦ Take a lot of family trips and outings. These don't have to be expensive adventures—sometimes a campout at the state park is more fun than anything. Making fun memories will cement your family together. We've taken a lot of trips—short and long—over the past twenty-one years. Sure, we'd have a big savings account if we hadn't spent the money on outings, but we'd rather be rich in memories. And spending your time and money on family activities tells your kids you care.

❦ "Sons are a heritage from the Lord, children a reward from him. Like arrows in the hands of a warrior are sons born in one's youth. Blessed is the man whose quiver is full of them. They will not be put to shame when they contend with their enemies in the gate" (Ps. 127:3–5). Thank the Lord for the privilege of having children. Ask him to help you be a good mother to them.

❦ Remind your kids regularly about how great they are. James smiles when I say, "If someone lined up all the seven-year-olds in the world and told me I could pick any one I wanted, you're the one I'd choose."

❦ "Practice yourself what you preach"—Titus Maccius Phutus.

Self-Disciplines

❦ Write your own principles for living. What do you want your children to know when they leave home?

8

Household Management for an Unmanageable Person

Sending your first-born child off to kindergarten is a big deal. Not so much for the child—who's growing weary of cartoon reruns—but for the parents. "Next thing we know he'll be in college," I sobbed. "This is a major turning point in his life." As it happened, John's kindergarten year was a major turning point in my own life.

Up to now, my idea of a disciplined morning schedule meant allowing myself to push the alarm snooze button only five times. (Any more than that would have been slothful.) John's first week of school made no difference.

I lingered under the covers until the last possible moment, then vaguely remembered that the tardy bell rings at 8:30. I rushed into John's room, jerked him out of bed, and threw some clothes on him. Then I hurried to the kitchen, dumped some Cheerios in a bowl, and reached into the refrigerator for milk. Oh great, I thought, this is not the day I needed to run out of milk. I'll have to try the old "lost in space" routine. Convincingly I said "John, I have a fun idea! Let's pretend our space ship crashed on the moon and we only have dried food to eat." "Mom," he calmly replied, "are you out of milk again?"

Watching him eat each bite of dry cereal in his typical methodical way, I grew more uptight by the second. "Hurry up, Honey, you don't have all day! Your car pool will be here any minute." I heard the horn, pulled him by the sleeve out the front door, and shoved him into my friend's car. She looked at me assuredly and said, "Don't worry, Kathy. The kids will be there on time. I'll use my radar detector." (Is it any wonder that other mothers avoided our car pool?)

I watched the yellow station wagon speed off—hoping John would have a good day at school. Reflecting back on my own elementary years, I remembered that school can be quite stressful for a child. I recalled how every class has its self-appointed bully whose destiny from birth is to verbally slice and dice other kids. "My baby!" I gasped and bit my knuckles. "He's out in the cold, cruel world . . . and I'm not making it any easier for him."

Luckily for my family, I learn fast. It didn't take me long to figure out our schedule had to change. At the rate we'd been going, we'd all have hypertension before Christmas break. Going as a family to use the take-your-own-blood-pressure machine at the drug store didn't sound like much fun.

I was ready to meet the challenge. Every morning I wanted my family to experience a peaceful, positive environment that prepared them to take on the pressures of the world.

But household management for an unmanageable person doesn't come easily. Feeling overwhelmed, I picked up my Bible and read the first chapter of Genesis. I gained a new sense of hope when I read that in the beginning the earth was formless and void—of any order at all. (My house fit this description. I read on.) After six days of work God saw all that he had made and said it was very good. Hmmm . . . , I thought. If he can take a chaotic mess and make something as beautiful and orderly as our world, I wonder if he would do the same for our home. I prayed and asked him to do this.

It didn't happen overnight. I began by praying myself out of bed in the morning. I didn't like getting up, so I just asked God to help me do it—not to make me like doing it. Then I figured out that I was at least part of the answer to my prayer. I was watching a lot of useless late-night television. I made the brilliant deduction that if I went to bed earlier then I might be able to get up earlier. Soon, I found that I liked being up before anyone else. It's funny how God answers our prayers in mysterious ways.

After I ran out of milk for the millionth time, it occurred to me that I might remember to buy it if I had written it down someplace. Okay, maybe I'm a slow learner sometimes. That was the beginning of my daily "to do's."

What I'm saying here is that it was a process, getting my morning schedule to be less hectic than it was. It was a cooperative project between God and me. And my family responded positively. They like seeing me cheerful in the morning. The boys like not having to rush around in the morning. And most mornings we have milk—and cereal—and juice—or something to eat for breakfast.

In the twelve years since I first prayed that prayer, we've come a long way. Mornings are my favorite time now—and actually the only quiet time in my day. I get up at 5:45, pour a cup of coffee, and enjoy some unhurried time with God. I read a chapter from the Bible and a devotional book, and write in my prayer journal. Then I putter at my desk and write down my daily "to do's." I've found that a list of everything I want to accomplish each day helps me stay focused. I tend to forget important items if I don't have a list in front of me.

After I write down my projects and errands for the day, I begin some household tasks. By the time the boys get up at 6:45, I'm ready to greet them lovingly and concentrate on creating an orderly atmosphere so they can start their day on a positive note.

When they leave for school at 7:50, I do fifteen minutes of housework. I wear tennis shoes and ankle weights so when I move briskly, I get some exercise at the same time. Then I dress and put on makeup, so that I'm ready to start work by 8:30. Even on the days when I don't leave my at-home office, I dress before I start work.

Now don't be too impressed. I may have the morning schedule under control, but there are other parts of my job as household administrator that make me glad I don't have to answer to a supervisor.

The dinner hour at our house is another story from a different book. Oh sure, the table is usually set in an enticing way with pretty dishes, colorful place mats, and cloth napkins. And our conversation is always lively as we recap the day and enjoy each other's company. But my cooking leaves a lot to be desired. Mainly a stomach pump. If there's ever a contest to find the world's worst cook, my family will make sure I'm a nominee. Even my neighbors harass me. When a fire truck roared down our street, they all ran to our house just sure I'd caught the kitchen on fire.

I thought my worries were over when Cajun cooking came into vogue. No cooking classes for me! No siree. I already knew how to fix blackened chicken, blackened round steak, and blackened chocolate chip cookies. But the kids weren't fooled. They still prayed regularly for God to intervene in the situation. They were not sure, though, how he would answer their prayer. They figured either he would give me a supernatural ability to cook well, or I'd sell enough books so we could order in regularly. They're leaning toward the latter since my becoming a good cook falls into the category of Red Sea miracles.

Actually my basic kitchen skills seem to be diminishing even as I write. Tonight at dinner Bill and the boys complained that their hands were extremely dry and smelled like chlorine. "Kathy, what kind of soap are you using in the sink dispenser these days?" he inquired. Preoccupied with the mind-taxing job of trying to get dinner on the table I answered, "I don't remember . . . the bottle's under the sink. Don't worry about it. Just carve the brisket."

As the boys cleaned up the kitchen, I heard a ruckus. Joel ran into the living room laughing hysterically. With more than a little sarcasm in his voice he said, "Mom, you're such a whiz in the kitchen. You put automatic dishwasher detergent in the hand soap dispenser. No wonder we've lost three layers of skin!"

Yes, the boys were cleaning up the kitchen. And it's to someone's credit—I don't know whose—that they know the difference between dishwasher liquid and hand soap. But it's to my credit—and Bill's—that they do participate in our household management. They live here after all. And I expect their future wives to thank me some day.

Nowhere that I know of is it written that Mom should be the handmaiden. Yes, it's important to make a healthy, welcoming home for everybody in the family. And I think it's just as important for everybody in the family to have some ownership in making the home. It's more than making sure the kids have regular chores to learn responsibility. When they help they feel the pride of "ownership" and the independence of being able to, in part and according to their age, take care of themselves. Plus if mine weren't doing the dishes they wouldn't have had that perfect opportunity to make fun of me—one of their favorite pastimes.

I also must confess my laundry expertise isn't anything to brag about. As a college freshman, the first time

I tried to wash my clothes, I put the detergent and my dirty clothes in the dryer. I couldn't for the life of me figure out how to turn the water on. Since then, I've improved only a little. Bill and I have endured some major marital conflicts over how many cotton shirts I've managed to shrink in the dryer. And I have an uncanny knack for washing the wrong colors together. John begs me not to touch his clothes. But I want to be a helpful mother, so I keep trying and hope he won't notice his athletic supporter has turned pink.

Sewing's not my department either. After I hemmed Joel's Sunday pants and stitched the left leg opening closed, the family voted to delegate all hemming projects to Bill. The older boys voluntarily signed up for homemaking in the eighth grade. Living around here, they knew they'd best learn a few basic survival skills.

Yes, Bill sews. And it hasn't made him noticeably less of a man. He learned as a young child by sitting and watching his mother sew. It comes in handy. Some families have a pretty traditional breakdown of chores around the house—she cleans and cooks; he takes the garbage out and takes care of the car. It may be, and usually is, the woman's responsibility to be the household manager. But husbands need to feel the same pride and independence that kids do. Now, I am NOT, NOT, NOT suggesting that you take this book and beat your husband over the head with it. Nowhere here does it say, "Kathy says you should do more around the house."

What it does say is that if you're feeling overwhelmed about managing your household, you have some resources to turn to. First, you can take your problems to God in prayer. That works wonders. Second, you can choose a time when the pasta isn't boiling over, the baby isn't screaming, you don't have house guests, and the taxes aren't due—surely there is one such half hour in your life—to talk with your husband sincerely, and without blaming, about how you feel. Perhaps you'll find that he wants to do more, but just doesn't know how to do it. Perhaps he feels like he'd be intruding on your territory if he tried to do things. Perhaps he feels like he's tried in the past and your standards were so high or you had such strong ideas about the "right" way for him to do something that he felt frustrated and scolded rather than satisfied for his effort.

Another responsibility I struggle with is keeping the house clean. Last month my kitchen got a four-star rating in *Housefly Monthly*. And I decided to give up vacuuming for Lent when James tracked in six inches of top soil from his dirt pile. It gave our carpet a tone-on-tone sculptured effect that wasn't half bad.

I don't even bother to clean some things, especially if it has been a long time since my last antidirt campaign. For instance, I don't even attempt to wash the gym shorts that have been in a wad under Joel's bed for six months. I use the broom handle to put them by the door so he can take them to school. His biology teacher loves to study new life forms, so he gets extra credit for bringing them in "as is." And I'm tempted just to board up the shower and forget about the grunge growing on the tile. After all, we have a garden hose in the back yard.

Yes, my family will unanimously report that "domestic" is not one of the words they use to describe me. But a pleasant, orderly environment is important to all of us, so I work on this constantly. I confess that since I now work full-time writing, speaking, and running a corporation, I have a housekeeper come in ten hours a week. But the rest of the time we're on our own. I'm always looking for shortcuts, easier methods, and fresh approaches to keep the household running effectively and efficiently. All five of us have busy schedules and need Home Sweet

Home to be a place we can count on for relaxation, renewal, and recreation. This means there has to be some semblance of order. It takes a lot of daily discipline to make this happen.

How many of you are old enough to remember the man who performed the plate-spinning act on the "Ed Sullivan Show"? One by one he spun china dinner plates that were balanced on top of long, thin rods. Just when he got number ten spinning, he had to run across the stage to rescue number one, which was about to fall. Then plates three and five almost crashed, and so on. We were a nervous wreck when he finally finished the act.

Many days that's exactly how I feel. I'm trying to balance being a wife, lover, mother, household administrator, chef, chauffeur, accountant, purchasing agent, teacher, and friend—while at the same time running Creative People, Inc., speaking, doing radio and television shows, writing and faxing magazine articles, and writing and promoting books.

When the demands seem overwhelming, I find hope and encouragement by reading about the woman in Proverbs 31. She was a multitalented diligent worker, not only at home, but also in her career and the community. In a day when women were considered baby factories, she executed several entrepreneurial ventures in real estate and textiles, while maintaining excellent management of her family estate. She obviously made very good use of her time. Although I have no theological basis, I'd be willing to bet she worked from a "to do" list! In order to accomplish so much, she must have been extremely focused. As busy as she was, though, she did not neglect her husband, her children, or her relationship with God. If he helped this woman keep her plates spinning, I pray he will do that in my life too.

Daily Disciplines

"When you cannot do as you like, the best thing is to like whatever comes your way. The secret of happiness is not in doing what one likes, but in liking what one has to do"—George MacDonald.

We all have to do things we don't like. And changing our attitude about doing them can sometimes make us like them. I refer you again to the miracle of Kathy getting out of bed in the morning. At first I did it because I had to. God helped me. And, then, one day, I found I liked doing it. It doesn't, of course, happen that we like doing everything we have to do. You hardly ever hear anybody say they like cleaning bathrooms. But we almost all like having clean bathrooms. And holding on to the knowledge that we like the result can go a long way in helping us change our attitude about what we're doing.

Remember lost hours and minutes add up. Time management experts tell us that 20 percent of our time brings 80 percent of the results. Conversely, 80 percent of our time is virtually wasted on just 20 percent of our results.

I offer you this list as a starting point. I don't expect it to solve your household management problems, especially overnight. (But if it does, be sure to let me know.) Remember, there's no right or wrong way to choose items on this list. Select the ones which appeal to you. Do some of them every day. Do some of them once. Save some of them for later. And when you're feeling particularly desperate, remember: You and God are in this together.

- ❦ Ask yourself some hard questions about how you spend your time. How much television do you watch? How much time do you spend on the telephone just chatting? Are there any other areas in your life where you might be wasting time?

❦ Make a list of the things you want to accomplish every day and leave blanks to write in items that vary. Make photocopies of your list and fill one out each morning.

❦ Get up thirty minutes earlier tomorrow morning and spend some quiet time alone praying and planning your goals for the day. (If you get up thirty minutes earlier for a year, you add seven and one-half days of awake time to your schedule.)

❦ Congratulate yourself at the end of the day for all the things you accomplished. Don't worry about what didn't get done. Just move those items to tomorrow's list.

❦ Listen to your biological clock and discover your prime time. What time of day are you at your best? When do you have the most energy? Do your most important work at that time. I'm at my best from 8:30 A.M. until 2:30 P.M. During those hours, I try not to do any mundane maintenance chores that could be accomplished when I'm not running at peak performance.

❦ When you work, work hard; when you play, play hard.

❦ Consolidate your errands and only do them on certain days. I shop for large quantity items once a month at a wholesale club. I shop for other groceries one morning a week at 5:30 (I can get my shopping done quickly and efficiently and do not have to wait in time-consuming check-out lines.) And since the boys drink five gallons of milk a week, I have it delivered to the house twice a week so I don't have to go back to the store.

❦ Make good use of small bits of time. Keep a stack of projects that you can work on when you have a few extra minutes.

❦ Reward yourself when you finish a hard task. Take time out to have a cup of tea or take a bubble bath in the middle of the day.

❦ Delegate whenever possible. You can't do everything.

❦ One day each month don't schedule anything. Just play soothing music and catch up at home.

❦ Don't go to the bank or post office from noon to two or on Friday afternoon. If you can't avoid the trip, take something to do or read while you're waiting.

❦ What would need to happen at your house for mornings to run smoothly? If getting up earlier than usual sounds impossible, figure out what you can do the night before to save time the next morning. Or maybe you need to go to bed earlier.

❦ Write in your prayer journal using the following quote to spur your thinking: "The wise woman builds her house, but with her own hands the foolish one tears hers down" (Prov. 14:1).

❦ Consider getting an answering machine or service. Turn it on when you have a lot of work to do. You won't be distracted by phone calls you can return later.

❦ Know what you're fixing for dinner by 9:00 A.M. Cook everything you can early. Late afternoon can be the most hectic time of the day.

❦ If you work outside the home, maximize the potential of your Crockpot and microwave oven. Set aside one day a month to cook in quantity and freeze.

❦ Don't procrastinate. When you have a distasteful job that must be done, make it as pleasant as possible. When I pay bills, I create a pleasing atmosphere so the job doesn't seem so bad. I brew interesting coffee, put fragrance oil on a light bulb ring, play my favorite classical music, sit near a sunny window, and write with my favorite pen.

❦ Shop during hours when others don't.

❦ Take periodic pleasure breaks during the day—even if it's only for five minutes. After working hard for two to three hours, stop and do something that you really enjoy. You can browse through a favorite magazine or catalog, read a chapter in a good book, take a quick catnap, fix a refreshing drink, reread a letter from a special friend, or whatever you like to do. You'll have more energy after your break.

❦ Keep paper and pen in your purse, your car, and beside your bed. Jot down spur-of-the-moment thoughts about items you need to buy or things you need to do. It's too easy to forget.

❦ Don't overdo. Everyone has a different capacity for work and stress. Pain is a good reminder that I'm overdoing it. When my hips and legs begin to ache, I know it's time to pull back and rest.

❦ "Well begun is half done"—Aristotle. Begin a new habit today.

❦ Wear a pretty apron if you hate to cook.

❦ If you can afford to eat out more often, do so.

❦ Ask yourself regularly, Is this the best possible use of my time?

❦ When writing in your prayer journal, ask God to help you administrate your household efficiently. This is one of my daily requests. I need all the help I can get.

❦ Save necessary household papers and warranties in colorful file folders. Keep them in an easy-access location.

❦ Eat a light lunch. A heavy lunch will make you sluggish.

❦ Always keep your tables set in an attractive way. When I see a pretty table, I'm motivated to cook a meal to eat there. Even the simplest meal can seem elegant at a nicely set table.

❦ When you feel overwhelmed with responsibilities, stop and ask Christ to make real in your life his invitation in Matthew 11:28: "Come unto me, all ye that labour and are heavy laden, and I will give you rest" (KJV).

❦ Make use of delivery and cleaning services. They cost a little extra, but can save you time and money in another area by freeing up your time.

❦ Let your children help with the housework even if their performance isn't quite up to your standards. It's good for them to help.

❦ Trade out chores with a friend with different abilities and gifts than yours. If you enjoy working in the yard, you can do the gardening for both homes. If she enjoys house cleaning, let her do the interior chores.

❦ Play peppy music while doing a task. You'll move faster.

❦ Be a self-starter. "Go to the ant, you sluggard; consider its ways and be wise! It has no commander, no overseer or ruler, yet it stores its provisions in summer and gathers its food at harvest" (Prov. 6:6–8).

❦ Pray with an attitude of thanksgiving while you're doing an unpleasant chore. You might thank God for the privilege of taking a shower daily with warm water while you're cleaning the shower stall. Or thank him that your family has clothes to wear while you're folding that mountain of clean laundry.

❦ Keep a project by the phone so you can work on it while talking.

❦ Don't eat sugary snacks for quick energy to get a job done. They will give you a quick rush, but you'll feel worse in the long run.

❦ Restock your cleaning supplies with colorful sponges and brushes, new dish towels, household cleaners, and anything else you need to clean your home efficiently.

❦ "Dost thou love life? Then do not squander time, for that's the stuff life is made of"— Benjamin Franklin. Do you ever squander time?

❦ "She watches over the affairs of her household and does not eat the bread of idleness" (Prov. 31:27). What does this verse mean to you?

❦ Don't be afraid to ask for help. Remember asking for help isn't nagging or making somebody else—your husband or kids—feel guilty. And people who ask for help aren't incompetent.

❦ Set your clocks five minutes ahead. You can always use that extra five minutes.

❦ Learn to just say no to requests and jobs that do not fit into your priorities and goals. A woman recently told me she has a t-shirt that says Just Say No. She wears it occasionally to remind herself she can say the N word. Remember you're always saying no to something . . . don't let it be your family.

❦ "The one quality which sets one man apart from another—the key which lifts one to aspiration while others are caught up in the mire of mediocrity—is not talent, formal education nor intellectual brightness—it is self-discipline"—Theodore Roosevelt. What is one self-discipline you would like to build into your life? Begin today.

❦ Remember that one thing we all have in common is twenty-four hours a day. It is up to me how I choose to spend it. If you're having trouble making choices, keep a time diary for a week. Record how you spend every waking fifteen minutes. Now, what do you want to change?

❦ "Sometimes when I consider what tremendous consequences come from little things . . . I am tempted to think there are no little things"—

Bruce Barton. What little things could mean big improvement at your house?

❦ When dishes and laundry seem like insignificant tasks, think about this: "The service of God is the service of those among whom he has sent us"—George MacDonald.

❦ Place fresh flowers near your kitchen sink to bring beauty to your work environment.

❦ Keep photographs of family members and good friends on your desk to bring you joy in the midst of boring paperwork. I have twenty-six frames on my desk.

❦ "A well-spent day brings happy sleep"— Leonardo da Vinci. Are your days well spent?

❦ Collect colorful office supplies to make household paper administration more fun. I keep multi-colored paper clips, pens, pencils, and file folders on hand.

❦ "Teach us to number our days and recognize how few they are; help us to spend them as we should" (Ps. 90:12 TLB). Look at each day as a gift from God. Ask him how he would have you spend it.

❦ Balance your work and play time. Researchers have found that play and leisure time help release built-up tension, can open blocked thinking and trigger creative ideas, stimulate an energy boost, and create hormones, endorphins, and other substances which activate your immune system.

❦ While we are busy with our plans and projects, God patiently reminds us, "I have spoken unto you, rising early and speaking; but ye harkened not unto me" (Jer. 35:14 KJV).

Self-Disciplines

❧ Remember the real challenge is not to manage your time, but to manage yourself. In order to begin managing yourself more effectively, ask yourself these questions: "What makes me feel energetic?" and "What drains my energy?" Make a list of these things. What can you add or avoid? What can you delegate? How can you work smarter? Keep your list here.

An Added Bonus: The Peel Spring
House-Cleaning Plan
(It doesn't have to happen only in spring.)

❧ When it's time to do a major house cleaning, start by surveying the territory. Begin at one end of the house and walk through each room with paper and pen. Write down all tasks that need to be accomplished in each room. Post the list in a prominent place. Ask your family to help. Letting everybody volunteer for what he or she wants to do helps ensure it'll all get done—and everybody gets to do something they like to do. Make it a first-come first-served contest to get the plum jobs. (And you've got to play. You don't have to do everybody's "don't wannas.")

❧ Make sure you have necessary cleaning supplies on hand. Put them in a basket so you can easily tote them from room to room.

❦ Start with one room and sort through each drawer, closet, and shelf. Ask these questions about each item:

a. Have we used it in the past year?

b. Does it have monetary or sentimental value?

c. Will it come in handy someday?

If your answer to a or b is no, throw it away or pass it on. Regardless of what your answer is to c, be ruthless and get rid of it. Next cleaning day you'll be glad you did.

❦ Carry a basket to pick up clutter and redistribute things to their proper place as you travel between rooms.

❦ Designate a special shelf to put items that need mending or fixing.

❦ Create receptacles to generally categorize the mounds of mail, magazines, and miscellaneous papers. (Don't get bogged down filing or reading today. Set aside another day to do paperwork.) Decide whether each item should go into the financial stack, things-to-do stack, family stack, or reference stack.

❦ Promise yourself you won't get sidetracked. Don't look through a box of old photos that you find under the bed or call a friend and tell her you found her scarf you borrowed three years ago.

Part 4

Confessions of a Desperate Disciple

9

In Search of a Godly Woman and Other Archaeological Expeditions

I was thrilled the first time I received an invitation to speak at a large convention. Just envisioning the marquee, the hustle and bustle of the crowd, and interesting people from all over the country caused a rush of adrenaline to flood my body. I had never been three thousand miles away from home for anything, and to think that I was actually on the program was almost more than I could handle. I started getting ready one month in advance. I wanted to be prepared!

After packing four days' worth of underwear, makeup, toiletries, and a few small appliances (hair dryer, hot rollers, curling iron, electric toothbrush, battery-operated manicure set, electric razor, travel coffeepot, alarm clock, and steam iron), I carefully placed twelve outfits with coordinating accessories in suitcases. When Bill had to rent a dolly to get my luggage to the car, I commented assuredly, "I want to be ready for any occasion." He had lived with me too long to argue.

When I arrived at the ticket counter with six bags, I tried to play it cool as I stood next to a covey of pin-striped Wall Street types who were giving me the once-over. One asked if he could help. "That's okay—I travel a lot," I flipped my head confidently, hoping he didn't notice that my twenty-five-pound shoulder bag had relocated my shoulder pad to my chest.

When the ticket agent told me I could only check three suitcases, I braced myself against the counter and tried not to faint. "I knew that," I lied, "I just wanted to give you the choice of which bags you wanted me to carry on."

Trying to look like a seasoned traveler, I made my way through the terminal and got to the gate just before my palms started to bleed. I readjusted my baggage, distributing the eighty pounds evenly. I hoped that I could make it down the aisle without beheading anyone. When I reached my seat I said a silent prayer of thanksgiving that the only victims lying in my path of destruction were a *Business Week* and one glass of champagne. Why, I closed my eyes and sighed to myself, didn't I become a hippie in college? No rollers, no razor, no responsibilities—and no money, I drifted back to reality.

I've always been one who likes to be prepared for everything and play the right role at every occasion. Just tell me what you expect of me and I'll try to meet those expectations. I don't want to be too talkative or too withdrawn, overdressed or underdressed, so as to draw attention to myself as being different or extreme. Freud would have had a heyday with my insecurities.

As the new wife of a "man of the cloth," my attitude was the same. I wanted to be the perfect counterpart. I fantasized about large churches having to take a number and stand in line to interview us. "Not only is this Peel fellow an excellent candidate himself," the chairman of the pastoral search committee would comment, "but have you met his wife? This godly man and woman would be such a blessing to our congregation."

Upon awakening from my daydream, I realized all I had to do was figure out how to be a godly woman. No sweat, I thought, I can do godly. Although it was hard to pin down the exact job description I needed to fill, I wasn't completely clueless. I knew my role probably included creating a wonderful Christian home for my children and being a good Christian wife to Bill. And in my heart I sincerely wanted to live a life pleasing to God. But it's a good thing I love a challenge—because I was blazing new territory.

What exactly was this Christian home? A small house? Big house? Does it have Christian plaques on the wall? Plaster-of-Paris praying hands on the table? What about a fish on the door? Does it have a television? Does the father sit in a straight-backed chair every night in front of the hearth and read the King James Bible to children who attentively hang on his every word?

And what about a good Christian wife? What does she look like? Does she wear makeup? Have long hair, short hair, permed or colored hair? Can she wear stylish clothes? Does she have a personality? Can she disagree with her husband? Is she allowed a career outside the home? Must she be an accomplished pianist, enjoy needlework, and have a file box filled with casserole recipes?

Years ago, I went to my first Christian women's seminar—legal pad in hand—and began my search for the godly woman. I had tunnel vision about finding one, because I was bound and determined to be just like her. I walked into the auditorium and began to work the crowd. The first group I introduced myself to looked like finalists in *Glamour* magazine's "Before and After" competition, who obviously hadn't made it to "After" yet. I made mental notes and moved on.

The next foursome I happened upon were sharing their secrets to stretching grocery dollars. One lady had come up with thirty-nine different ways to serve pinto beans. I tried to appear fascinated.

Then I heard laughter coming from the other side of the room and decided to check it out. I found a group of lively women obviously having a good time. They were so regular I figured they must be *irregular*. They couldn't possibly be godly women. One remarked that she and her husband had been to the theater last weekend. Another talked about being active in her college sorority alumni group. I really liked these gals, but I figured they couldn't be candidates for godly women. They were too stylish and were having too much fun. Too bad, I thought. They must be here for the same reason I am.

I accumulated quite a long list of possible characteristics, and during the next four years I tried to become what I thought was a godly woman. I let the frosting grow off my hair and stopped wearing eye liner. (I hoped God wouldn't mind a little mascara.) I stored my good jewelry, threw away my sexy underwear (to my husband's dismay), and bought a woven bun holder for my hair. I gave away my colorful clothes and bought boring, neutral outfits. I vividly recall walking into a department store to buy a new pair of shoes. My eyes caught a pair of classy heels. I silently reprimanded myself for being so magnetized by something so impractical. "What I need is one pair of plain, black, all-purpose shoes," I rationalized. I bought them—and secretly hated the sight of them.

I closely watched a missionary's wife and tried to model her lifestyle. She had short hair, so I cut my hair short. She was a perfect housekeeper, so I almost killed myself trying to keep my house spotless. She was an excellent seamstress, so I tried to make curtains. I drew blood every time I picked up a needle. Quite frankly, I can't remember a more miserable time in my life.

About this time I began to hear trickles of gossip coming down through the ranks of the church we attended. Two women paid a visit to my home. One said she felt it was her duty to inform me that some thought it was a poor Christian witness for me to belong to social organizations that were not Christian in nature. "Why would you want to spend time with so many non-Christians?" she asked pointedly.

"Funny," I tried to hide my perplexity, "but didn't Jesus hang around with nonreligious types like prostitutes and tax collectors?"

"And while we're on the subject of your image," the other lady interjected, "we suggest you stop answering the phone in such a jovial manner. You sound like such a fake."

I held back my tears and thought to myself, Maybe I'm not supposed to be so happy about life.

"I'll try to tone it down," I compliantly responded aloud.

"Why, God," I cried out when they left, "did you choose me to be your child, then handicap me so that I can't be what I'm supposed to be? I can never be a godly woman. I just don't fit the bill."

Still searching, I joined a Bible study led by older women. These women were attractive, intellectually astute, and spiritually on the ball. They also were each quite unique and comfortable in their differences. They seemed to know God in a way I hungered to know him. They studied and taught God's Word in their own manner, reverenced and respected their husbands, prayed faithfully for their children, and were involved in various spheres of influence in the community. They had a perspective about life and a grip on reality that I craved.

It became clear to me that in my pursuit to become a godly woman, I had attempted to be someone I wasn't. Actually I had created sort of an alien being—combining one lady's taste in clothes with another gal's hair style and trying to copy one woman's gifts and talents with still another's personality and convictions. I was a glorious mess! After trying so hard to conform to the standards and tastes of others, I began to see I am a one-of-a-kind work of art, unlike anyone else who has ever lived or ever will.

My excitement grew as I saw that God loves variety, and I am the only person on the face of the earth who possesses my particular tastes, gifts, talents, and personality. I wondered why it took me so long to understand that all of God's creation praises him by just being what it was created to be. In Psalm 98:8–9, I read, "Let the rivers clap their hands, let the mountains sing together for joy; let them sing before the Lord."

"Of course," I finally comprehended, "how do the rivers praise God? By being rivers! And how do the mountains praise God? By being mountains!" I felt totally relieved.

What a comfort to be released from the burden of trying to be someone I'm not! Now I craved to know not what clothes, hair style, or mannerisms I needed to incorporate into my life to play the right role. Instead I sought how I could best live a life pleasing to God, given the gifts, talents, and background he gave me. For only I have the authority to express the gospel through my unique gifts.

I began an in-depth study of the New Testament—not out of obligation, but as an act of love to the God who created me, loves me unconditionally, and patiently deals with me. I wanted to know how to please him and best bring glory to him. In the first chapter of Colossians I found four results of a life pleasing to God.

1. Bearing fruit. Manifesting the fruit of the Spirit—love, joy, peace, patience, kindness, goodness, faithfulness, gentleness, and self-control (Gal. 5:22–23).

2. Growing in the knowledge of God. Not just knowledge about God, but knowing him as a person.

3. *Being strengthened.* Experiencing God-given strength that produces endurance and patience in the midst of trials and temptations.

4. *Giving thanks to the Father.* Having an attitude of joyful gratitude in all circumstances.

"And we pray this in order that you may live a life worthy of the Lord and may please him in every way: bearing fruit in every good work, growing in the knowledge of God, being strengthened with all power according to his glorious might so that you may have great endurance and patience, and joyfully giving thanks to the Father" (Col. 1:10–12).

I desperately want these characteristics to describe my life. I have a *long* way to go, but I want to live a life worthy of the Lord. So these four qualities are my goal. I don't aspire to them because God is holding a bat over my head saying, "You'd better be like this—or else!" But I strive because I want to please him out of gratitude for what he has done for me. It's incredible to think there's nothing I can do to make God love me more, and there's nothing I can do to make him love me less.

Understanding that God loves me as I am has helped me figure out where I went wrong in the first place. I wanted someone to tell me exactly what to do—what role I was expected to play daily if I'm trying to obey God. This desire was the driving force behind my search to come up with a list of specifications. The only problem was that in my quest to discover how to be a godly woman, I went to the wrong source. I learned that many people want to clone disciples rather than help them express who God created them to be. Had I gone to God and asked him what he wanted, I would have learned that he demands two things: a relationship and faith. No list about what to wear, what to eat, or how to look is involved.

God doesn't tell us how to answer the telephone. And he doesn't accuse us of being phony if we sound cheerful. God wants us to be happy. By growing closer to him, I become more like him and learn to think his thoughts. I can then understand how he wants me to express my unique personality for his glory and my love to my husband, children, neighbors, and the world. That's what "bearing fruit" is.

But just like an apple tree cannot strive, grunt, then force fruit from its branches, I cannot put bearing the fruit of the Spirit on my "to do" list each day—as something I'm determined to accomplish. The characteristics of God listed in Galatians 5 appear in my life in much the same way fruit appears on a tree. After being planted in good soil, nurtured, fertilized, watered, and exposed to light, over time fruit is borne. As I try to expose myself regularly to a spiritually nurturing environment and feed myself regularly from God's Word, over time I begin to see signs of some fruit of the Spirit.

The key words here, though, are "over time." And there's one big lesson I have learned over the years about growing closer to God and bearing fruit. It takes time—something we baby boomers are short on. We grew up in the world of instant gratification. We're into microwave cooking, jet travel, one-hour film processing, and ten-minute lube jobs. I even get impatient waiting for a document to come through my fax machine. It's all too easy to let this mentality transfer over to my relationship with God. Sure I want a relationship with God. Of course I want the fruit of the Spirit to characterize my life. My problem is I want instant Christlikeness the same way I want a quick tan—rub on the lotion, then wait an hour.

Through a process which I believe, by faith, but do not completely understand, God is at work in my life. In Philippians 1:6 Paul writes, "He who began a good work in you will carry it on to completion until the day of Christ Jesus." As I regularly spend time with God through prayer, reading and studying his Word, trying to practice his presence, and striving to obey his principles, he transforms me into his image. In the same way a close friend's mannerisms rub off on me, his character traits show up in my life at unexpected moments in exciting and surprising ways.

I also am amazed that as I gradually grow in my relationship to God, I discover new strength—strength to say no to temptation, to endure hard circumstances, to hold my tongue, and to desire his will instead of mine. In areas where I once was weak, he makes me strong.

And slowly, but surely, as I get to know God in a deeper way, I learn I can trust him more. This allows me to relax and to give thanks in more and more situations, and to accept with joyous gratitude the way he created me.

Finally, I grasped the simple truth that being a godly woman is just *being* the person God created me to be— and expressing his likeness through my unique qualities as I seek to know and obey him. Kind of a paradox—I'm free to be me as I grow to be like him.

Daily Disciplines

"I am responsible for the depth of my message. God is responsible for the breadth of my ministry"—source unknown.

I like this quote because it gives me perspective. It particularly gives me perspective when I'm running around like a chicken with its head cut off, trying to spread the good news as far abroad as possible. The message gets pretty thin when I'm trying to be all things to all people—only God can do that. I get frustrated and other people (not surprisingly) get cranky when I try.

If I want to be a godly woman, all I'm responsible for is developing my relationship with God—getting to know him—and me, in the process—better and better each day. If I do that, he'll let me know what ministry he wants me to do—where, when, and how.

Most of the disciplines in this section are therefore about getting to know God and growing deeper in relationship to him. We can't do that without devoting time to it. It seems like if we devote time to our prayer and spiritual life, other things start taking care of themselves. We know what we're supposed to do, and, miraculously, we have time and energy to do it.

Pick and choose the disciplines that work for you. Please, please, please, don't try to do them all at once. Remember, God has given you time, and deep relationships only develop over time.

- ❧ "The fear of the Lord is the beginning of knowledge" (Prov. 1:7). It helps me to think of "fear of the Lord" as moment by moment awareness that God is always with me, and as I practice acknowledging his presence, I will strive to make wise choices instead of foolish ones. How would your life change if you were constantly aware of God's presence?

- ❧ "Understanding is the reward of obedience"—George MacDonald. Is there something you feel you should do, but don't want to? Sometimes discerning God's presence and leading can be muddled if there is an area of blatant disobedience and sin in my life.

- ❧ Get involved in a good Bible study. We will never know God through a superficial understanding of his Word.

❦ A godly woman is one who lives out that which she cannot explain through her unique God-given personality and gifts. Get to know yourself. God made you just the way you are for his purpose. Only you can fulfill that purpose.

❦ Genuine knowledge of God reveals itself in a transformed character. This happens not only because we are in the Word, but because we let the Word get in us. Don't just fill your head with Bible knowledge. Ask God to apply his word and its transforming power to your heart.

❦ Begin a spiritual life notebook. Use it to write down prayer requests, insights you receive from studying the Bible, and inspirational quotes from sermons and other books.

❦ Do you have friends who encourage you spiritually? If not, ask God to give you some. If you do, go see them.

❦ "Give ear and come to me; hear me, that your soul may live" (Isa. 55:3). Spend some quiet time daily listening to God with your heart. What righteous impressions and passions do you feel?

❦ Don't forget God is always nearer to you than anything or anyone else. Not talking to him every day is like not talking to your children every day.

❦ Read a Psalm aloud as an act of worship to God. Some psalms may express your feelings better than you can.

❦ "Be still before the Lord and wait patiently for him" (Ps. 37:7). Is your life ever really quiet—

so that you can just sit, wait, and listen for
God?

❦ Try to read a portion of God's Word every
morning so you won't forget to start the day
without trusting in the life-causing God.

❦ Take time to practice patience with yourself.
Cut yourself some slack. Be patient when you
don't do everything on your list or when it
takes you longer than you think it should.
Take a break.

❦ Study people in the Bible. You will find that
God uses sinful people of all types to do his
work.

❦ Try to read one chapter of Proverbs every day.
I have done this fairly regularly for twenty-
two years, and each morning I still learn
something new.

❦ In order to make sure you get a chance to
practice joyful gratitude, include at least one
thing that gives you pleasure in your daily
schedule. It is surely pleasing to God that
we're thankful for facials or bubble baths, for
instance.

❦ "One main test of our dealings with the world
is whether the men and women we associate
with are better or worse for it"—George
MacDonald. What kind of example are you
setting for others? Do you want to change it?
Ask God to help you.

❦ Make a list of the fruit of the Spirit you want
to manifest in your daily life. Yes, refraining
from commenting on your husband's old

sweatshirt is manifesting a fruit of the Spirit—self-control.

❦ "Our grand business in life is not to see what lies dimly at a distance, but to do what lies clearly at hand"—Thomas Carlyle. God's will is to do what he has put around us.

❦ Buy a modern translation of the Bible that is easy to understand. A good concordance and Bible commentary are also helpful. Ask a staff person at a local Christian bookstore to help you.

❦ God handpicked you to be his representative to your generation. He wants to bring about change and wants you to be one of his critical instruments. If you could say anything at all to the world, what would it be? Make a list. Then make a list of how you can do some of these things right now—yes, today—in your life.

❦ Read *The Complete Green Letters,* by Miles Stanford. This is an excellent book about the basics of the Christian life.

❦ Be true to who God made you. "This above all: to thine own self be true; And it must follow, as the night the day, Thou canst not then be false to any man"—William Shakespeare.

❦ Worship regularly at a church that refreshes you spiritually. You will receive more if you go prepared to worship. If you cannot find a church that meets your needs, go simply to worship. God is pleased when we worship him. (See Heb. 13:15–16.)

❦ Listen to the Bible on cassette tapes while driving. Hebrews 4:12 says God's Word is alive—working in our lives although we cannot feel it.

❦ Memorize your favorite Scripture verses and passages. This is extremely hard for me, but I am surprised how much the verses I have memorized help me when I am in difficult situations.

❦ Remember you are "called of God" no matter what your vocation. Seventy-five percent of the prominent spiritual heroes of the Bible were lay men and women.

❦ "But you are a chosen people, a royal priesthood, a holy nation, a people belonging to God, that you may declare the praises of him who called you out of darkness into his wonderful light" (1 Pet. 2:9).

❦ Always be on the lookout for spiritual role models—people you can learn from and look up to as an example.

❦ People will always question what you do. If you're following God's leading, expect some flak.

❦ You are who you are, when you're alone in the dark. How you choose to spend the idle moments of your time says a lot about you.

❦ Confess your sins regularly and specifically to God. No matter what you have done, he lets you start over.

❦ Your imagination is a God-given gift. Use it to visualize yourself doing what you know would be Christlike behavior.

❦ Try reading a year-old devotional Bible. I like *Time with God: The New Testament for Busy People.*

❦ Make notes in your Bible when you are studying a passage. This will be helpful to you later.

❦ Remember your worth to God in public is what you are in private.

Self-Disciplines

❦ "I have come that they may have life, and have it to the full" (John 10:10). Take some time to begin a list of ways this verse can affect your life. What areas of your life would you like him to fill up?

10

How Desperate Are You?

Some people become missionaries in Africa to have a cross-cultural experience. Others join the Peace Corps. We moved across Dallas.

After our gala Ken-and-Barbie wedding—Bill was afraid he'd need to *hire* groomsmen when I told him he'd need fourteen friends—we packed the rental trailer with enough silver and china to serve a six-course seated dinner to Congress.

Our financial statement looked pretty impressive for a couple of newlywed college seniors. We lived in a nice apartment near the SMU campus. We owned two cars, our college tuition was completely paid, and my parents continued to send me $150 every month for allowance. (That was quite a bit of "disposable income" in 1971.) Frankly, we didn't know how good we had it.

But I should have known our cushy lifestyle wouldn't last forever. We graduated from college, Bill enrolled in seminary, and our parents cut the apron strings. But not to fear . . . we were excited about our new adventure! We had never experienced poverty before. After all, who needs money when you're young, in love, and living for Jesus?

Besides carrying a heavy study load, Bill worked as the youth pastor at a local church. I taught school part-time.

I also played Russian roulette with my birth control pill dispenser. John was born five days before our third anniversary.

When I tell you that we had no money, I mean we had no money. By the time we paid graduate school tuition, baby bills, and basic living expenses, we were flat broke. We had a checking account, but the balance was zero.

I need to add that my mother was feeling very sorry for us by now. And so, in her sweet and generous way, she wanted to help us out. She tried to turn our musty, old rented house into a home. Home, that is, as I once knew it. She sent money and made me promise to spend it on a housekeeper—which wasn't exactly a line item in our budget.

Since I had a dog growing up, she thought it would be nice for Bill and me to have one. So she bought us a poodle. Everything you are thinking at this very moment about poodles was true of Nanette. She was fidgety, temperamental, fuzzy, and she had bad breath. Since we could hardly afford to buy food for our family, we didn't relish the thought of buying food for this dog. But we did, and she became a member of our family.

One weekend after visiting Bill's parents, we pulled into our driveway and began unloading the car. I noticed something protruding from our mailbox. It was a book— *The Oral Roberts Book of Miracles*. We walked inside the house, and as we opened the book, twenty-dollar bills flew out of it. We counted $300 while staring at each other in amazement.

Bill, wonderful man of integrity that he is, said that we'd have to find out where the money came from. I, on the other hand, completely dismissed any virtue that may have been resident within me and thought, This guy's too honest for his own good. I blurted out, "Bill, who cares where the money came from? Just let me go to the store!"

He won the argument. We put the $300 back in the book and left to teach a Bible study. It was here that we learned the origin of the gift. Two boys in our youth group saved the money they earned from their summer jobs. Wanting us to experience a miracle, they gave us all their money in *The Oral Roberts Book of Miracles*. We were overwhelmed with their love and generosity. But we had to tell them we could not accept the money because they did not have their parents' approval.

When we returned home, we found *The Oral Roberts Book of Miracles* on the floor with its binding chewed to shreds. Cash was strewn all over the living room. We scolded the dog and began to pick up the money. All we could find was $280. We were twenty dollars short. Puzzled, we turned and looked into the face of a very guilty poodle. You guessed it. She had eaten a twenty-dollar bill.

Never before, nor ever since, has my husband been so angry with one of God's living creatures. "Now, not only are we broke," he sighed, "we're twenty dollars in the hole, and I've got to give the money back to the kids." Bill looked at me, I looked at him, then we both looked at the poodle. "A man's got to do what a man's got to do," he stated with resolve.

For the next two days my desperate husband followed the dog around the yard with my kitchen colander and the garden hose. (I'm going to leave parts of this story to your imagination. Rest assured that whatever you're thinking is probably true.)

He retrieved two-thirds of the twenty dollar bill. It was quite discolored. We carefully glued the pieces together on a piece of white paper and took it immediately to the bank to trade in for another. The teller suspiciously stared at me and said, "I'm not going to ask you where this bill has been." I just smiled, went straight home, and threw away the colander.

That event is not on our list of most favorite early marriage memories, but it taught us a big lesson. At times, the circumstances in our lives must get pretty bad before we realize that we're desperate. Sometimes it takes extreme discomfort to turn things around, to break a bad habit, to heal a relationship, to forgive someone, to build discipline into our lives, or to search diligently for answers from God. But I'm convinced, beyond the shadow of a doubt, that desperation is a great place to be.

The Bible says that God cares intimately about the details of my life and desires my fellowship. (Read Psalm 139:13–18.) But most of the time it seems I am too wrapped up in my own little world to remember this. I think he must tenderly smile to see me hit the point of desperation—whether personally, emotionally, financially, relationally, or spiritually. He tells me to call on him: "Call to me and I will answer you and tell you great and unsearchable things you do not know" (Jer. 33:3). And, when I do, I'll get results. "Then they cried to the Lord in their trouble, and he saved them from their distress" (Ps. 107:13).

I guess I'll always be calling and crying to the Lord for one thing or another when I get desperate. My life never lacks difficult circumstances. Some of these situations are the consequences of poor choices. Other problems are completely out of my control. It seems like I get one area of my life somewhat in order when catastrophe breaks loose in another. More days than not my life seems to be—as Bill's dad used to put it—"in a mell of a hess." That may seem like a severe way of putting it, but many days that's exactly how I feel. But God always meets me at my point of desperation in unexpected ways.

Recently I found myself unable to see how God would work out a difficult situation. I felt so alone—and so desperate. Trying to hold back the tears, I got in my car to run errands. I turned on the tape player thinking perhaps music would minister to my troubled spirit. The boys had left "Go West Young Man" by Michael W. Smith in the player. It was cued to the line, "When you're up against the wall, you know I'll be there—for you, for you." The tears started to flow. "That's how I feel, Lord— up against a wall," I said aloud, not caring if anyone saw me supposedly talking to myself. As I cried and sang along with the tape, God helped me turn the song into a prayer of thanksgiving—thanking him in advance that he would be there for me.

One day my stress was so intense I left dinner cooking in the oven and went to a place I have discovered where I can see the sun set. I hoped that somehow God would speak to me through his creation. That evening he painted a beautiful sunset across the western sky that reminded me of Colossians 1:16: "For by him all things were created: things in heaven and on earth, visible and invisible." I knew if he is the creator of everything and in control of the universe, he is big enough to handle my problems. I left and returned home with new strength to keep going.

Another time God used a chorus of birds singing to bring me joy in the midst of pain. Depressed over a sin I couldn't seem to gain victory over, I laid down on the living room floor. I was embarrassed that I had to come before God once again with the same sin he had heard about so often before. As the birds flew in from the east and perched outside my window, they began to sing. After about five minutes of melody, they flew away toward the west. My heart suddenly overflowed with joy as I remembered: "As far as the east is from the west, so far has he removed our transgressions from us" (Ps. 103:12).

In another instance, God guided my thoughts and led me into victory amidst a desperate situation. When I found myself struggling even to want to fight sinful thoughts and behaviors, I prayed, "Father, I am so desperate I don't even know where to start." I am convinced the Holy Spirit brought to mind the plan of action I wrote down in the middle of the battle:

1. Acknowledge the problem.
2. Confess the problem to God.
3. Correct any behaviors that could be causing the problem.
4. Reconfirm my commitments that affect the problem.
5. Renew my thoughts with God's Word about the problem.

As God helped me follow through with these actions, a potentially destructive situation turned into a spiritually enriching experience.

I've found that my ability to turn to God and receive his help amidst desperate situations has a lot to do with my spiritual state of mind. If I have been seeking to walk with God, learn his Word, and obey his laws—trying to fill my mind with good things—I am quicker to ask for his help, see his answers, and respond to his leading. But, on the other hand, if I have been seeking to please myself, walk independently of God, and not wanting or trying to obey him—filling my mind with thoughts I know are wrong— I become spiritually sluggish and find it hard to respond wisely and seek his help in hardship. In *Ordinary Christians in a High-Tech World*, Robert Slocum told a story that perfectly relates my feelings about this problem:

"I recall a university student who encountered the claims of Jesus and, on the spot, committed his life to Christ. He returned to his usual routine in the dorm, classroom, and social life. After a few weeks, he met with his Christian counselor, who asked him how things were going. He said, 'It's like there is a black dog and a white dog inside my life and they are fighting all the time.' The counselor asked him which one was winning. The student thought a moment and replied matter-of-factly, 'The one I feed the most.'"

When I regularly "feed the white dog," turning to God in time of need is a natural response. When I have been "feeding the black dog"—although I feel desperate—I am embarrassed to turn to him. But when I finally do turn my red eyes toward heaven and tell God I am a desperate woman in need of his help, in some way he lets me know that he understands and will never give me more than I can bear: "No temptation has seized you except what is common to man. And God is faithful; he will not let you be tempted beyond what you can bear. But when you are tempted, he will also provide a way out so that you can stand up under it" (1 Cor. 10:13). When I am in a place of desperation, forced to hold my hands out to heaven for help, God stands there ready to give. Actually he was standing there all along, but I was too busy or proud to accept his help.

Although I've made a diligent effort to discover the source of this poem, I've been unable to. I share it with you in spite of that (and not intending not to give credit) because it says it best:

> One by one he took them from me
> All the things I valued most;
> 'Til I was empty-handed,
> Every glittering toy was lost.
> And I walked earth's highways, grieving,
> In my rags and poverty,
> Until I heard his voice inviting,
> "Lift those empty hands to me!"

Daily Disciplines

"As Christians we have the past, the pleasant and the future. Our past is absolutely forgiven, our future is absolutely certain, so that, more than any other body of people on the face of the earth, we are free to live in the 'pleasant tense'"—Tim Hansel.

Of course, when we're in the present it may not always seem so pleasant. It's not that, as Christians, everything will go the way we want it to—that we won't have fights, accidents, setbacks, desperate times of one sort or another. God doesn't expect us not to have desperate times. He does expect us to turn to him in them, though.

Our past is forgiven. All we have to do to be forgiven is ask. Then we can let the past be past. Sure we can take our lessons from it. We can learn from our mistakes and our failings. And we may have to live with the consequences of them. But, in a very real sense, we don't have to live with them. God has forgiven us. Can we do less for ourselves?

And our future is certain. There is promise after promise in Scripture to that effect. As long as we stay with God, he'll stay with us. In fact, he'll stay with us even when we seem, in our desperation, to turn away from him. (See Josh. 1:5.) We can always come back, and our future is certain.

If we only trust that we live with a forgiven past and a certain future, we can live with more assurance in the present. If things go wrong, we can take them to God. If we believe, a way will open for us.

The disciplines in this section open the way to living in the present with God—every day. They aim at getting us up and getting us going, in our best direction, the direction God has ordained for each of us. Pick the ones which apply to your life right now. Know that you can come back to others later. Why not take a moment right now to start. He's waiting for you.

- ❦ Cry out to God if you feel desperate. "Listen to my cry, for I am in desperate need" (Ps. 142:6).

- ❦ Keep a prayer journal. Write down your deepest feelings. This will help you clarify your thoughts.

- ❦ It's not what happens to us but our response to what happens to us that hurts us. How have you responded to hurtful circumstances? Is that how you really want to respond?

- ❦ "Pain is inevitable; misery is optional"—Tim Hansel. What are you choosing to be miserable about? Sometimes just acknowledging my part in choosing to be miserable is the beginning to seeing my situation in a more positive light.

- ❦ When difficult things happen in my life, I say aloud, "For this I have Jesus." It reminds me of his presence and his strength to get me through the hardship. I learned this from a sermon by Dr. John Hunter.

- ❦ No matter what you have done, no matter how desperate you are, God will meet you at your point of need. Remind yourself of this, twenty times a day if need be.

- ❦ "Jesus Christ's life was an absolute failure from every standpoint except God's. But what seemed failure from man's standpoint was a tremendous triumph from God's, because God's purpose is never man's purpose"—Oswald Chambers. Although your circumstances may cause you to feel like a failure, remember God has a purpose in mind for you.

❦ Spend some time outside. Crush leaves under your feet, lay down in a field of wildflowers, climb a mountain, watch a sunset, or sit by a lake. Ask God to reveal himself to you through his creation.

❦ Do something for a friend who is in a desperate situation. This will help you as well as your friend. When I was going through a difficult time, a dear friend took me to Dallas to a lovely hotel just to get away from it all. Her husband even kept the kids. I came home refreshed.

❦ "It is the man who is conscious of his own impotence as a believer who will learn that by the Holy Spirit he can lead a holy life"—*The Complete Green Letters,* by Miles J. Stanford. I wrote this quote in my journal when reading this book. Later, during a desperate situation, I wrote beside it, "Lord, I feel totally impotent." I was encouraged to remember that it's okay and perfectly human to feel impotent, and it's only with the Holy Spirit's help that I can lead a holy life. Is there an area in your life where you are conscious of your impotence? Acknowledge it and let God help you.

❦ "That which we obtain too easily, we esteem too lightly"—Thomas Paine. The intangible treasure we have at the end of a desperate situation is priceless. Know that something good will come out of what you are going through right now.

❧ What areas in your life are you ready to do something about now? Write down your thoughts and the date. Tell a close friend who will hold you accountable.

❧ "I can do everything through him who gives me strength" (Phil. 4:13). With Christ's strength I can be responsible or "response-able." Is there a response you need to make in a certain situation? God will make you able.

❧ I am what I am today because of the choices I made yesterday. What choices can you make today that will make you who you want to be tomorrow?

❧ Ask your pastor, a Christian counselor, or a trusted friend to help you through a desperate situation.

❧ Read books by Max Lucado. They will give you hope and insight into how much God cares about you.

❧ Faith is acting like it's so when it's not in order for it to be so. How can you act out your faith today?

❧ How exactly are you asking God to meet your needs in your desperate situation? Sometimes he answers my prayers by giving me what I ask for. Other times he answers by just helping me get by without what I asked for. Like Garth Brooks sings, "Sometimes I Thank God for Unanswered Prayers." A lot of times what I ask for, I don't need at all.

❧ Read one Psalm every day. Write down at least one verse that is meaningful to you.

❧ Think about this and take comfort: "When you pass through the waters, I will be with you; and when you pass through the rivers, they will not sweep over you. When you walk through the fire, you will not be burned; the flames will not set you ablaze" (Isa. 43:2).

❧ Proactively change anything in your power that may be complicating a difficult situation.

❧ "God delights to increase the faith of his children. We ought, instead of wanting no trials before victory, no exercise for patience, to be willing to take them from God's hand as a means. I say—and say it deliberately—trials, obstacles, difficulties, and sometimes defeats are the very food of faith"—George Mueller. There are days when I cry out to God, "Please Lord, I don't think I can stand for my faith to grow much more." I wonder if I will ever be so close in my relationship with God that I will willingly take trials from his hands—knowing he means for them to build my faith in him. Can you see how he has stretched your faith through trials and defeats?

❧ When you feel depressed, start a project. Work is very healing and helpful.

❧ Find a prayer partner and regularly pray together. This will give you strength.

❧ In order for God to help us, he asks for our time, attention, and affections. The "cares of this world" are his stiffest competition. Give God at least a few minutes every day.

❧ Write down insights to Scripture verses and the date in the margin of your Bible. When I go through tough situations, I write down how various verses strengthen and help me. It is a delight to look back later and see how God worked.

❧ Don't let a day go by without praying alone. Remember that God understands: "For we do not have a high priest who is unable to sympathize with our weaknesses, but we have one who has been tempted in every way, just as we are—yet was without sin. Let us then approach the throne of grace with confidence, so that we may receive mercy and find grace to help us in our time of need" (Heb. 4:15–16).

❧ Join a fellowship or support group of like-minded people.

❧ Don't be afraid, no matter how desperate your situation. There are 350 passages in the Bible that tell us to "fear not." Finding and reading them is a good way to deal with fear. You may even want to record them in your prayer journal for quick reference.

❧ When going through a dark passage in life, fill your mind with truth. Don't fall prey to illegitimate forms of escape.

❧ "The great thing in this world is not so much where we are, but in what direction we are moving"—Oliver Wendell Holmes. In what direction are you moving? Do you want to turn around? Do it now.

❧ Get away and rest. Stressful situations can be exhausting emotionally, physically, and spiritually. After intense circumstances in his life, the prophet Elijah felt afraid and weary. He even prayed he might die. Then he slept and an angel brought him food and drink. He slept again. This strengthened him and he was able to get up and travel forty days and forty nights.

❧ Our first response to adversity should not be to try to remove it, but to allow it to reveal our true weaknesses. This is hard—but necessary.

❧ Don't forget God is always nearer to us than anything else.

❧ "Live as you will have wished to have lived when you are dying"—Christian Furchtegott Gellert. Do you have regrets? Do something today to rectify them.

❧ The method that God uses to save us out of our distresses is his word. "He sent forth his word and healed them, he rescued them from the grave" (Ps. 107:20).

❧ "Mishaps are like knives that either serve us or cut us as we grasp them by the blade or the handle"—James Russell Lowell. Can you apply this to a circumstance in your life?

❧ God's ultimate purpose in getting our attention is to conform us to the image of Christ. On the basis of this purpose, all adversity works together for our good (Rom. 8:28–29).

❧ What do you perceive as limitations in your life? "That which appears to us to be a limitation can actually become our unexpected advantage and asset. As we are forced to our knees once again, we discover the holy and wonderful gift of life"—Tim Hansel.

❧ Read the Book of John. Write down the verses that bring you comfort.

❦ "Get up and go on" is a friend's favorite phrase to use when she feels like a failure. Ask yourself, What's one way I can get up and go on today? Then get up and go on.

❦ Are you waiting for something miraculous or magical to happen in your circumstances? What can you do to make things better? "Nothing will ever be attempted if all possible obstacles must first be overcome"—Samuel Johnson.

❦ Collect inspirational music. Music is the language of the soul.

❦ Memorize your favorite Scripture verses. They will be a comfort to you during difficult times.

❦ "Adversity causes some men to break; others to break records"—William Ward. How do you see yourself responding to adversity?

❦ If you were an outside observer on your life, how would you see yourself responding to hardship? "It is difficulties that show what men are"—Epictetus.

❦ A mistake is a failure only if you fail to learn from it. What have you learned lately?

❦ Read *A Shepherd Looks at Psalm 23,* by Phillip Keller. You will understand in a deeper way how God takes care of you.

❦ "Most people live their life indefinitely preparing to live"—Paul Tournier. What will you do in the next twenty-four hours that will keep you from being part of this sad fact?

❦ "Never, never, never, never give up"—Winston Churchill.

Self-Disciplines

❦ Remember God is merciful. "May your mercy come quickly to meet us, for we are in desperate need" (Ps. 79:8). Jot down things, ideas, prayers, verses, and quotes from books that God has used to comfort you. How has he shown you his mercy? How has he met your needs? Learn to look for his hand at work in your life. He cares about your every need and every detail of your being—even down to the hairs on your head. (See Luke 21:18.)

11
Now It's Your Turn

I started this book knowing I was a desperate woman—and suspecting there were others like me. I also started, as I said in the introduction, with the sure knowledge that I have what all other desperate women have:

1. a heavenly Father who has begun a good work in me and, despite my sinfulness, is absolutely committed to transforming my character into the likeness of Jesus Christ,

2. a living Savior who has promised to be my daily deliverer from sin's dominion,

3. an indwelling Holy Spirit who empowers me to do God's will,

4. the promises in God's Word that guide me to know what is excellent,

5. fourteen hundred and forty minutes each day in which I choose how I'm going to live, and

6. enough problems to keep me challenged on a daily basis.

The disciplines in this book have helped me work out my ongoing life and my growing relationship with God who makes it possible for me to go on even though I'm desperate. Some of the most amazing things happen when I turn in desperation to God. I'd like to share one more.

I can't stand *just* to cook dinner. After starting the main course, I try to write a paragraph, return a phone call, and run a quick errand. My family knows the smoke alarm buzzer is the usual signal for dinner. Actually, they marvel at my strange compulsion to do two or more things at once. I drive them nuts trying to accomplish twice as much in half the time.

The same goes for driving a car. Since the invention of cruise control it seems such a waste of time just to *drive*. I've learned to take notes while listening to books on cassette and totally redo my makeup at the same time. (It was during this procedure I learned the importance of watching for potholes while applying mascara.) I've also become quite adept at performing calf-strengthening exercises while styling my hair at seventy miles per hour. I lose consciousness for only a few seconds after saturating the air with hair spray. After riding in the car with me, you'll understand why faith in God is such an important part in the lives of my children.

On one particular day in August, I behaved in my usual manner. As I began a two-hour business trip to Dallas to meet my agent, I wanted to make the most of my drive time. Wishing for the day when cars come equipped with autopilot, I set the cruise control, turned on a Mozart tape, and pulled out some scratch paper and a pen. I balanced it on top of the combination armrest/ storage box/writing surface next to the driver's seat in my car. This is a good time to work on my goals, I thought. It seems I've never gotten out of the school-year mode of thinking, so I still operate on a September to August basis. I started this discipline about ten years ago

at the advice of a friend who is a time management con-
sultant. I've found it helps to write out what I would like
to accomplish in a year and how I would like to grow in
various areas of my life. This helps me stay on the path to
where I really want to go.

As is my custom, I divided my life (and my paper)
into seven categories. There's nothing particularly ingen-
ious or spiritual about my divisions, they just work well
for me. As I traveled the familiar road to Dallas, I
scribbled these goals for the coming year:

Intellectual

> Read three books a month
> Learn one new vocabulary word each
>   week
> Learn how to use our new computer

Physical

> Aerobically exercise four times a week
> No sugar, white flour, and ten chips
>   per week
> Exercise arms with weights three times
>   a week
> Apply lotions and creams to skin twice
>   daily

Spiritual

> Daily write in prayer journal
> Read one Proverb daily
> Study through the Books of Mark and
>   James

Family

> Praise Bill and each boy for at least one
>   thing daily
> Show affection to Bill and each boy
>   daily

Create a warm, fun atmosphere
morning and night
Administrate household well

Social

Write at least one thank-you note each
week
Plan something fun to do with another
family once a month

Professional

Sharpen speaking skills (Meet with
speaking coach. Listen to two tapes
a month of excellent speakers and
write down what I can learn from
them.)
Spend twenty hours each week writing
and promoting books
Deliver more than I promise

Just for Me

Get a manicure twice a month
Master my favorite classics on the
piano
Look my best every day

After I finished my list, I read back over it and shook my head. Then I wrote this prayer at the bottom of the page:

Father, I believe that because you created all of life, then all of life is spiritual. I sincerely want to be an excellent wife, mother, professional, and disciple, but there is no way I can even come close to accomplishing these goals and daily disciplines. I ask for your help, Lord. I am a desperate woman.

"Of course!" I shouted as I reached the Forney exit, "a book for desperate woman." I knew immediately this was the women's book God wanted me to write.

Tears streamed down my cheeks. Today I feel deep joy when I see the results of God's work and that prayer.

I hope that you will use what you like from this book to set a plan for yourself. It can be for three months, a year, however long. It should inspire and stretch you. It should be about all parts of your life. Maybe using my categories, maybe making up your own. The words from the song by Joni Eareckson Tada, "The Part You Wrote for Me," seem particularly pertinent and I share them with you here. Whatever it is, it should reflect who God made each and every one of you to be.

> I play so many games; I have so many faces.
> I've run so many races
> That need not be run by me.
>
> I talk so many ways; I know so many stories.
> I sing so many ballads
> That need not be sung by me.
>
> O Lord, dear Lord, great author of the play,
> May I in wisdom learn,
> The only part that I need play
> Is the part that You wrote for me,
> The part that You wrote for me.
>
> You give me the lines;
> You show the right direction.
> You gave me a reflection of what I need to say.
>
> So many want to leave,
> And so many times I follow.
> Lord, let me not be hollow,
> Like men in those other plays.
>
> O Lord, dear Lord, great author of the play,
> May I in wisdom learn,
> The only part I need to play,
> Is the part You wrote for me;
> The part You wrote for me.

God wrote a part for each of us. When we discover that part, it is easier to keep on track in our lives. Daily disciplines and setting goals can help us get in touch with the part God intended for each of us to play and help us stay focused on that part. More importantly, over time, we stay in touch with God and with the real person—ourselves—he meant us to be.

I once read, "If you aim for nothing, you'll hit it every time." I believe there's a lot of truth to that statement and we must regularly ask ourselves the questions, "What do I really want to do? What are the desires of my heart? Where do I want to go in life?" As one *desperate woman* to another, these questions and their answers are critically important. I am forced to think when I read this passage from *Through the Looking Glass*, by Lewis Carroll:

> "Would you tell me, please, which way I ought to go from here?"
> "That depends a good deal on where you want to get."
> "I don't much care where."
> "Then it doesn't matter which way you go."

For a reason which I cannot explain, God has placed a passion in my soul to help women understand which way they ought to go. I see this as encouraging them to strive for excellence and become all God created them to be. I feel very strongly that this is one purpose he has for me during my stay on planet earth. I pray, that in some small way, this book has partially fulfilled this purpose. I would be thrilled to know you have been encouraged to begin some daily disciplines in your life. I also hope that perhaps you have seen yourself in a new light—one that exposes your true beauty and uniqueness as God's work of art. And I hope that you have seen your Creator in a new way—as one who loves you personally, cares intimately about every detail of your life, and has a unique purpose for your life that only you can fulfill.

I sincerely believe you will benefit from this book if you make it your book. Write in the margins, underline principles you want to remember, turn down the pages, jot down ideas that come to mind, and add your own unique twists to the applications. Make it about your life—and then write to me. I'd love to hear from you!

Kathy Peel
Creative People, Inc.
P.O. Box 5100
Tyler, Texas 75712